gemeinsam
Friedenschluß.

○

reichlich
finanziell
unterstützung
und
einverständnis
unsererseits.
daß
Mexico.
in
Texas
①
Neu
Mexico.
①
AR
IZ
ON
A

5454
16102
15217
22801

GARY BLACKWOOD

MYSTERIOUS
MESSAGES

A HISTORY OF
CODES AND CIPHERS

DESIGNED AND ILLUSTRATED BY JASON HENRY

•• DUTTON CHILDREN'S BOOKS ••
an imprint of Penguin Group (USA) Inc.

For Ingram
—G.B.

DUTTON CHILDREN'S BOOKS
A division of Penguin Young Readers Group

PUBLISHED BY THE PENGUIN GROUP

Penguin Group (USA) Inc., 375 Hudson Street, New York, New York 10014, U.S.A. • Penguin Group (Canada), 90 Eglinton Avenue East, Suite 700, Toronto, Ontario M4P 2Y3, Canada (a division of Pearson Penguin Canada Inc.) • Penguin Books Ltd, 80 Strand, London WC2R 0RL, England • Penguin Ireland, 25 St Stephen's Green, Dublin 2, Ireland (a division of Penguin Books Ltd) • Penguin Group (Australia), 250 Camberwell Road, Camberwell, Victoria 3124, Australia (a division of Pearson Australia Group Pty Ltd) • Penguin Books India Pvt Ltd, 11 Community Centre, Panchsheel Park, New Delhi - 110 017, India • Penguin Group (NZ), 67 Apollo Drive, Rosedale, North Shore 0632, New Zealand (a division of Pearson New Zealand Ltd) • Penguin Books (South Africa) (Pty) Ltd, 24 Sturdee Avenue, Rosebank, Johannesburg 2196, South Africa • Penguin Books Ltd, Registered Offices: 80 Strand, London WC2R 0RL, England

Text copyright © 2009 by Gary Blackwood

CIP Data is available.

Published in the United States by Dutton Children's Books, a division of Penguin Young Readers Group
345 Hudson Street, New York, New York 10014 • www.penguin.com/youngreaders

DESIGNED BY Jason Henry
Printed in China • First Edition
ISBN: 978-0-525-47960-4
1 3 5 7 9 10 2 6 4 2

The fact that you've picked up this book probably means that, like me, you're fascinated with codes and ciphers. But I could be wrong. Maybe you're not the least bit interested in them—or *think* you're not.

Even so, give the book a chance. You'll find that cryptography—the art of creating secret messages—is far more than just an intellectual exercise for eggheads. Codes and ciphers have played a major role in some of the most important events in history. They've brought about the downfall of kings and queens, changed the course of wars, decided the fates of countries.

But cryptography isn't the exclusive property of sovereigns, soldiers, and spies, either. I'd be willing to bet that, no matter how cryptologically challenged you are, you've used a secret code more than once, and so has everyone you know.

Sound like an exaggeration? Not at all.

Have you ever stopped a friend from saying something stupid by making silent gestures behind the back of a third person? Maybe you made a zip-your-lip motion, or silently formed the words *Shut up!* Or maybe you kicked your friend's shin under a table, or rolled your eyes, or gave a warning look, or just surreptitiously shook your head. Those are all secret codes of a sort.

Did you ever convey what you meant without actually saying it, just by giving your friend a hint and then adding, "You know what I mean." Secret code again. Ever given someone a wink on the sly, to let that person know you're just joking? Secret code. Have you ever ordered an item online that was paid for with a credit card? Then you used a secret code.

Computer cryptography is a relatively recent development, of course, but those other types of codes, or something very much like them, have been around literally for ages—long before the concept of zippers, even before there were tables to kick people under.

Ever since humans first learned to communicate, they've been finding ways of doing so in secret. It wasn't until the development of written language, though, that they began to come up with truly clever and complex methods of concealing their messages.

· Contents ·

CHAPTER ONE

Clay, Wax, and Greece

1500 BCE – 100 BCE

The first known example of cryptography is inscribed on a clay tablet dating from roughly 1500 BCE. It's not one of those ciphers I mentioned that played a major role in history. It's a formula for making pottery glaze.

The symbols are similar to the ones used in cuneiform, the world's oldest system of writing, which originated in Sumer (now southern Iraq) around 3000 BCE. The unknown potter used a stylus made from a reed or a piece of wood or bone to press the symbols into a damp clay tablet, then dried the clay. But to make sure his secret glaze recipe stayed secret, he altered the cuneiform symbols or used them in unusual ways. According to cryptologist David Kahn, a rough equivalent in modern English would be playwright George Bernard Shaw's playful spelling of *fish* as

FODB, ZDA, DQG JUHHFH

Sumerian vase (c. 2400 BCE)

Examples of cuneiform script

GHOTI—using the *GH* from the word *tough*, the *O* from *women* (pronounced "wimin"), and the *TI* from *nation*.

After this benign beginning, the art of cryptography took a more sinister turn. In the fifth century BCE, the countries and city-states of the Near East and Southern Europe seemed to be in continual conflict. In a war-racked world, it's not the artisans who most need to keep their messages confidential. It's the military. But back then warriors were, by and large, not a very literate bunch. "At a time when it was still a major accomplishment for even an educated man to be able to read," says author Brian Innes, "thoughts had not yet turned to codes and ciphers, and man's ingenuity was directed to ways of hiding the written messages."

Putting a message down in *plaintext*, or ordinary writing, and then somehow concealing it, is called *steganography*, and some of the methods that military commanders and their spies came up with really were ingenious.

During the centuries-long conflict between Greece and Persia, one Greek secret agent used as his messenger a slave with a sore leg. He bound a poultice of healing herbs around the man's wound. His reports on the enemy's plans were written on the leaves.

Herodotus

Greek,
484–425 BCE,
first known
historian

The Greek writer Herodotus—often called the father of history—recounts a gory technique used by a nobleman named Harpagus: He slit open the belly of a freshly killed rabbit, hid his message inside, and sent it off with a courier posing as a hunter.

Histiaeus, a Greek who lived at the Persian court, used a bizarre method of steganography to incite his countrymen to rise up against the Persians. Apparently he was in no hurry to start the revolution, for he shaved the head of a trusted slave, tattooed his seditious message on the man's scalp, then waited for the hair to grow out before sending the slave off with instructions to shave his head again once he got to Greece. The communication sparked a rebellion that lasted six years.

· The Boring Definitions Box

Instead of bogging things down with a bunch of boring definitions, I'm going to stick the most important ones here, in a box by themselves, where you can consult them if you need to and ignore them if you don't.

Cryptography is the art of writing messages with a hidden meaning.

Cryptanalysis is the art of figuring out those hidden meanings.

Cryptology is the study of cryptography and cryptanalysis, including the study of codes and ciphers. Those two terms are sometimes used interchangeably, but to be accurate: A **code** is a method of secret writing (codes are usually written, though there are also visual and spoken codes) in which an entire word or phrase is replaced by another word or phrase, or by a group of letters or numbers. For example, in a 1920s business code, the group **YBDIG** means "plundered by natives." Seriously.

A **cipher** replaces each individual letter of a message with a different letter or a number or possibly a symbol, so the word "natives" might read ***%#ꝏȿ+!**, like a cartoon curse word.

In these examples, "plundered by natives" and "natives" are the plaintext; the code group **YBDIG** and the symbols ***%#ꝏȿ+!** are called the ciphertext. All the ciphertext in this book will be in **bold** print; plaintext will always be in ordinary print.

In *The Histories*, Herodotus relates how the cunning use of steganography helped save Greece from being conquered by the Persian king Xerxes. When the city-states of Athens and Sparta refused to pay tribute to him, Xerxes assembled a huge army and a fleet of warships and, in 480 BCE, descended on Greece. A Greek named Demaratus, living in exile in Persia, dispatched a warning to Sparta, using a writing tablet covered with wax so that letters could be pressed into it. But, as Herodotus explains:

> since the danger of being discovered was so great, Demara-
> tus . . . took a pair of tablets, and clearing the wax away from
> them, wrote . . . upon the wood whereof the tablets were
> made; having done this, he spread the wax once more over the
> writing . . . When the tablet reached [Sparta], there was no

one . . . who could find out the secret, till Gorgo, the daughter of Cleomenes and wife of Leonidas, discovered it, and told the others. "If they would scrape the wax off the tablet," she said, "they would be sure to find the writing upon the wood."

Gorgo's cleverness had a downside, however. Her husband led a small force of Spartans to defend the pass at Thermopylae, hoping to delay the advance of the Persians. Though they did buy their countrymen some time, the Spartan soldiers paid dearly for it; they were wiped out to a man.

When Xerxes' navy reached Greece, the Spartans and Athenians were ready for them. With newly built warships of their own, they surrounded the Persian invaders in the Bay of Salamis and soundly defeated them.

The military-minded Spartans also developed the world's first apparatus for enciphering and deciphering messages. In typical no-frills Spartan fashion, it consisted of only two simple elements: a wooden staff or baton called a *scytale* (sit-a-lee), and a long strip of leather or parchment. The sender wrapped the strip around the scytale in a spiral, then printed his message on it. When the strip was unwrapped, it seemed to contain a meaningless string of letters—

A Relief sculpture of the Persian king Xerxes.

FODB, ZDA,

until the receiver wrapped it around another staff of the same size.

In 404 BCE, a bloody messenger stumbled into the quarters of a Spartan general named Lysander, removed a leather belt, and handed it over. The belt was embossed with seemingly random letters. But when Lysander wound the belt around his scytale, a message materialized: the Persians, it said, were planning yet another attack. Thanks to the warning, Lysander stopped the enemy before they reached Sparta.

The scytale method wasn't really very secure (see sidebar), and lasted only about a century. But the ancient Greeks invented other forms of encipherment that remained in use for over two thousand years. Their codes and ciphers had a major influence on the development of secret communications.

A Greek historian known as Aeneas the Tactician was the first scholar to expound on the subject of cryptography. His treatise *On the Defense of Fortified Places*, written around 350 BCE, introduced a clever form of steganography. The sender opens a bound book (or, in Aeneas' day, a scroll) and, with the point of a pin, makes tiny holes, invisible to the casual reader, beneath selected letters. When the receiver holds the page up to the light, the pinpricked letters spell out the message. In the fourth century BCE, when books were scarce, the method wasn't all that practical, but in today's literate society it's a simple and relatively secure way of communicating in secret.

SIDEBAR | How to Create (and Solve) a Scytale Cipher

Nowadays, a good scytale is hard to find. Luckily, you don't need a genuine scytale in order to encipher a scytale-style message. All you need is the cardboard tube from a roll of paper towels and a continuous strip of paper. The strip should be a half inch wide and between two feet and eight feet in length, depending on how extensive your message is.

Tape one end of the paper strip to the tube at a slight angle, then wrap it snugly around the tube in a spiral—the way you'd wrap tape around the handle of a baseball bat or a hockey stick. Print your message lengthwise along the tube, one letter to each row of the paper strip, leaving no spaces between words. If you need more room, turn the tube an eighth of a turn and print another line.

Unwind the strip and you've got a series of letters that make no sense except to somebody with an identical tube—or to somebody who knows how to decipher the message without a tube. If you read on, you'll be one of them.

Sculpture of a
Spartan soldier

FODB, ZDA, DQG JUHHFH

The scytale cipher is a transposition cipher; it has all the same letters as the plaintext (the original message) but they're jumbled up. To demonstrate, let's use a simple cryptogram, or enciphered message:

WST EPH AEE PAW OKI NTS SOE

Print the first letter in each group, then the second letter in each group, and so on, and you get:

WEAPONSSPEAKTOTHEWISE

a quote from Pindar, a Greek poet who lived in the age of the scytale.

(Warning: This method works only if the sender was considerate enough to make all the lines in the message the same length. The sender also has to wrap the paper strip in the proper direction—toward himself, rather than away—or the ciphertext will read backward.)

In the mid-1800s, Edgar Allan Poe, the famous writer of mystery and horror stories, suggested another method of solving a scytale cipher. Form a long, narrow cone out of cardboard; wrap the cipher strip around it and slide it up and down the cone until you find a spot where the letters line up to form words.

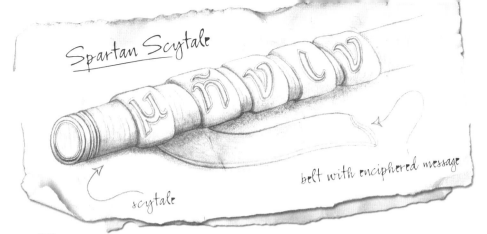

Spartan Scytale

scytale

belt with enciphered message

Two centuries or so after Aeneas, another Greek historian took a giant cryptological leap forward when he invented an enciphering system that still bears his name. With the Polybius checkerboard (also known as the Greek square), you can create a fairly sophisticated *substitution cipher*; instead of just jumbling up the plaintext letters, this cipher replaces them with a whole different set of letters or symbols or numbers. Naturally, Polybius used the Greek alphabet, but here's a checkerboard using the English, or Roman, alphabet:

	1	2	3	4	5
1	a	b	c	d	e
2	f	g	h	ij	k
3	l	m	n	o	p
4	q	r	s	t	u
5	v	w	x	y	z

Since the letter *s* is in row 4, column 3, it's enciphered as **43**. The letter *u* is **45**. Give it a try. See how quickly you can enci-

FODB, ZDA, DQG JUHHFH

pher the phrase "winged words" (a quote from the Greek poet Homer).* You can make the cipher a little harder to crack by printing the letters in the checkerboard in random order.

The Greek square was the model for a host of later ciphers, usually written ones. But apparently Polybius saw it as a way to send visual signals over long distances, using flaming torches. Nobody's sure exactly how the system worked, but the sender could conceivably have held, say, two torches in one hand and two in the other to represent the number **22** or the letter G. Imagine, though, how hazardous it would be trying to juggle enough torches to make a Z!

By Polybius' time, Greece was no longer a major military power. Like most of the lands that bordered the Mediterranean, it had become part of the ever-expanding Roman Empire. Rome had begun to invade the world of cryptography, too, over which Greece had held a virtual monopoly for nearly five centuries.

* 52 24 33 22 15 14 52 34 42 14 43

CHAPTER TWO

The Rise and Fall of Rome

100 BCE – 500 CE

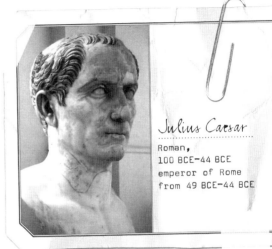

Julius Caesar

Roman,
100 BCE–44 BCE
emperor of Rome
from 49 BCE–44 BCE

During his campaign to conquer Gaul (now France) the Roman general Julius Caesar communicated with his officers using the Greek alphabet, which to an uneducated man would have seemed like . . . well, like Greek. In *The Battle for Gaul*, Caesar tells how he sent one of his Gallic cavalrymen to deliver a message to the commander of a Roman fort surrounded by hostile tribes:

> I wrote the letter in Greek characters, so that if it were intercepted the Gauls should not discover what our plans were. I told the man that if he could not get into the camp, he must fasten the letter to the thong of his spear and then throw this inside the rampart.

WKH ULVH DQG IDOO RI URPH

Unfortunately, the spear stuck in one of the towers of the fort and hung there for two days before the besieged soldiers noticed the message and learned that help was on the way.

Caesar also devised a simple but enduring substitution cipher. According to the second-century writer Suetonius,

> he changed the order of letters in such a way that no word could be made out. If somebody wanted to decipher it . . . he had to insert the fourth letter of the alphabet, that is D for A, and so on.

To use the Caesar cipher, just print the regular alphabet and, beneath it, print a second alphabet that starts with **D** instead of **A**:

a b c d e f g h i j k l m n o p q r s t u v w x y z
D E F G H I J K L M N O P Q R S T U V W X Y Z A B C

The letter "j" is enciphered as **M**, "w" is enciphered as **Z**, and so on. Here's a brief cryptogram for you to solve. The plaintext is something Caesar himself supposedly said as he led his army into Rome in defiance of the Senate, which had ordered him to resign.

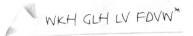

WKH GLH LV FDVW*

The art of steganography, which had been pretty crude as practiced by the Greeks (remember the dead rabbits and the tattooed scalp?), was refined considerably by the Romans. In *The Art of Love*, written about 1 BCE, the poet Ovid counsels lovers to keep their correspondence secret by using a form of invisible ink:

Tithymallus plant

A letter . . . escapes the eye when written
in new milk; touch it with coal dust and you will read. That
too will deceive which is written with a stalk of moistened flax,
and a pure sheet will bear hidden marks.

Roman scientist Pliny the Elder recommended using the milky juice of the tithymallus plant, which became clear as it dried. When held over heat, the sap turned brown.

● ● ●　● — — ●　● —　— ● — ●　●

Western Europeans weren't the only ones experimenting with cryptography. The Greeks' old enemies the Persians created a substitution cipher that replaced the letters of the alphabet with the names of birds, and another that used astrological symbols.

Though China had a written language as far back as 2000 BCE, it didn't lend itself very well to encipherment because, instead of an alphabet, it used ideograms—symbols that represent ideas or objects rather than letters or sounds. A Chinese diplo-

　　　　WKH ULVH DQG IDOO RI URPH

° The die is cast.

mat or military leader who wanted to send a covert communication usually just had his courier commit it to memory. That method had an obvious drawback: The courier could be bribed or tortured into spilling the beans.

One alternative was to write the message on a thin piece of paper or silk, roll it into a tight ball, and coat it with wax. When the wax cooled, the messenger hid the object in his clothing, swallowed it, or concealed it—in the words of the fifteenth-century writer Machiavelli—"in the most secret places of the body."

One of the few systems of Chinese cryptography was developed by women in the county of Yongjiang sometime in the third century. Most Chinese women of the time didn't lead very pleasant lives. Their marriages were arranged; they were denied an education; some suffered the agony of foot binding, a process meant to keep their feet small and delicate.

These women could express their sorrow and frustration only to other females, and only in secret. To help them do so, they created a cryptic form of writing called Nushu, or "women's script." To prevent the system from being discovered, after reading a message in Nushu, the recipient burned it.

Chinese characters   Nushu script

Women in India—upper-class women, at least—had considerably more freedom. They were actually encouraged to learn a variety of arts and skills. A fourth-century text, the *Kama Sutra*, instructs women in sixty-four different disciplines, or yogas, including music, lovemaking, magic, bookbinding, chess, carpentry, and cryptography—presumably so they could communicate in secret with their lovers. The book suggests pairing up the letters of the alphabet at random to create a substitution cipher, as in this example (which uses the English alphabet and not the original Sanskrit):

a	t	f	k	s	b	y	h	m	n	e	o	u
j	w	q	c	g	l	i	v	d	z	p	r	x

To encipher or decipher a message, just replace each letter with the one directly above or below it.

In the fifth century, European cryptology—and all other branches of learning—suffered a major setback. The Roman civilization, already weakened as it was and split into the Byzantine and Western empires, collapsed under the onslaught of the so-called barbarians—German tribes that included the Visigoths and Vandals. With the fall of Rome, Europe descended into what is known as the Dark Ages

WKH ULVH DQG IDOO RI URPH

[og] Ham and Bacon

500 CE – 1412 CE

Some historians apply the term *Dark Ages* to the period beginning with the fall of Rome and ending in the year 800, when Charlemagne, king of the Franks, was crowned emperor of the West. Others extend the Dark Ages into the tenth century. Still others include everything up to the dawning of the Renaissance in the early fourteenth century. This implies that for nine centuries or so, Europe was a sort of intellectual wasteland.

There's no denying that the period was one of wars, invasions, and political turmoil. But despite all that, scholars and scientists went on writing and studying and speculating. Even the "uncivilized" Celtic tribes of the British Isles weren't totally ignorant or illiterate. They had a distinctive writing system of their own, called ogham (pronounced *oh*-am). The ogham alphabet looked

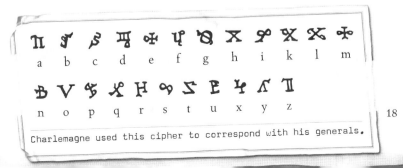

Charlemagne used this cipher to correspond with his generals.

18

something like this (I've made it correspond to the English alphabet so you can use it as a cipher):

h d t c q b l f s n m g p z r a o u e i/j k v w x y

In actual use, ogham was written vertically, not horizontally. Though it wasn't meant as a form of cryptography, it got used that way. A fifteenth-century Irish text called the *Book of Bally-mote* lists a dozen methods of enciphering ogham, including reversing the alphabet, replacing each letter by the next one in the alphabet, and a variation called "the outburst of rage ogham," in which one letter is substituted for another seemingly at random.

According to legend, as the ancient Celtic hero Bres was about to go into battle, he received a secret message written in an unusual form of ogham and got so caught up

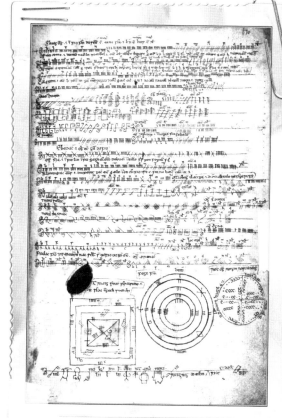

A page from the *Book of Ballymote*

ᛅ ᛒ ᚲ ᛏ ᛁ ᚠ ᚠ ᚷ ᚷ ᛁ ᚠ ᚠ ᛚ ᛘ ᚼ ᚻ ᛒ ᚢ ᚱ ᚴ ᛏ ᚢ ᚠ ᚾ ᛁ

a b c   d   e f   g   h i j   k   l m n   o p q   r   s   t u/v w   y z

Runes (above) were the written language of Germanic tribes in the Dark Ages, but were also used later by scribes and priests as cryptograms.

in trying to decipher it that he lost the battle. This method is known as "the ogham that bewildered Bres."

In later centuries, cryptography would become an essential tool for ambassadors and other diplomats. In Medieval Europe it was still mainly a weapon of war. Occasionally, though, it was used in a more playful fashion. A ninth-century Irishman named Dubthach, living in exile at the court of the king of Wales, created a cryptogram that he challenged every visitor from Ireland to solve. Apparently, he held some grudge against his countrymen and wanted to prove how stupid they were.

Dubthach wrote a message in Latin, then enciphered it in Greek, confident that "no Irish scholar, much less British" could decipher it. But three traveling Irishmen solved the cipher, then sent the solution home for the benefit of "such of our simple and unsophisticated Irish brethren as may think of sailing across the British sea, lest perchance otherwise they might be made to blush in the presence of . . . the glorious king of the Britons, not being able to understand that inscription."

Scholars found another valuable use for cryptography—to conceal controversial ideas and opinions. The medieval church had little tolerance for anyone who questioned the established order. New scientific theories and experiments, in particular, risked being labeled heresy or black magic.

Thirteenth-century Franciscan friar Roger Bacon, imprisoned for speculating about such "dangerous novelties" as gunpowder, flying machines, and telescopes, declared that "A man is crazy who writes a secret unless he conceals it from the crowd . . . so that it can be understood only by effort of the studious and wise."

In his *Epistle on the Secret Works of Art and the Nullity of Magic*, Bacon suggested seven ways of concealing ideas, including writing down only the consonants in a word; mixing in Hebrew, Greek, and Latin letters; and writing in some form of *ars notaria*, or shorthand. In the centuries that followed, some famous historical figures would make use of Bacon's methods, among them astronomer Galileo Galilei, chronicler Samuel Pepys, and poet Geoffrey Chaucer.

Notice that all the substitution ciphers I've mentioned so far—the Caesar cipher, the Polybius checkerboard, the *Kama Sutra* system, even enciphered ogham—are *monoal-*

Roger Bacon
English, 1214–1294, philosopher and Franciscan friar.

phabetic; each letter of the regular alphabet is always represented by the same letter or symbol or number in the ciphertext. For example, in Caesar's system, the letter "e" is always enciphered as an **H**. Even today, the average person will find a monoalphabetic cipher hard to solve; in an age when most people weren't even literate, the method was relatively safe.

Then, in the early fifteenth century, Egyptian cryptologist Shihab al-Qalqashandi delivered a crippling blow to the monoalphabetic cipher, destroying once and for all its illusion of security.

For several centuries, Muslim scholars had been aware that, in any text, some letters appear more often than others. A few had speculated that this fact could be used to help decipher encrypted messages. In a treatise he wrote in 1412, al-Qalqashandi explained exactly how:

> *When you want to solve a message which you have received in code . . . count how many times each symbol is repeated and set down the totals individually. . . . When you see that one letter occurs in the message more often than the rest, then assume that it is alif [a]; then assume that the next most frequent is lam [l].*

Once you have the most common letters in a ciphertext figured out, it's a fairly simple matter (see sidebar) to solve the rest. This technique, called *frequency analysis*, was a real boon for cryptanalysts.

Making Mincemeat of a Monoalphabetic Message

As you can tell from al-Qalqashandi's name, *alif* and *lam* are the most frequently used letters in Arabic. To get a rough idea of the most common letters in English, look at a Scrabble game: You get ten points for using a Z or a Q, and only one for using an A or an E. Arrange the letters according to how often they appear in writing, and you get something like this (depending on what text you use for the frequency count): E T A O N I S R H L D C U P F M W Y B G V K Q X J Z

Here's how you use that frequency chart to solve a monoalphabetic substitution cipher. Remember that this won't work on a transposition system like the scytale cipher, or on a *polyalphabetic* cipher, which uses several substitutes for the same plaintext letter. Naturally, a sentence with a lot of rarely used letters in it—for example, "Quentin quickly questioned zany zombies"—fouls things up, too.

The method works best on a long cryptogram, but for demonstration purposes I'll use a brief quote from Chaucer:

M HJCQLMKS HZOIL JMRI Z JIMDS OIK HIGG HJMH
HJIDI ZL ACN ZK JIMRIK MKS VMZK ZK JIGG

The most frequent letter here is **I**, so
let's assume that stands for **E**. Replace all
the **I**s with **E**s and you get some groups that
begin to suggest words, such as **HJEDE**. What's
the most common five-letter word that has **E**s
in those positions? THERE.

Replace all the **D**s with **R**s, the **H**s with **T**s
and the **J**s with **H**s and **HJMH** turns into THMT—
undoubtedly THAT. So all those **M**s are really
As. If the **Z** standing there by itself is not
an A, what else could it be but an I? So are
all the other **Z**s. The three-letter word **AKS**
is most likely AND, so turn all the **K**s into
Ns and the **S**s into **D**s. Now the ciphertext
looks like this:

A THCQLAND TIOEL HARE I HEARD OEN TEGG
THAT THERE **IL ACN** IN HEAREN AND VAIN IN HEGG *

The rest is a piece of cake. **IL** has to
be IS, and **THCQLAND** must be THOUSAND, which
makes **ACN** into A0N, and **TIOEL** into TI0ES, or
TIMES, which makes **OEN** into MEN. Since the
last words in each line obviously rhyme, it's
pretty clear what they are. It's a small step
from HARE to HAVE and from HEAREN to HEAVEN.

* A thousand times I have heard men tell/That there is joy in heaven and pain in hell.

What's in heaven? Can't be GOD in this case, since we know the cipher letter for D is S. How about JOY? And what's in hell? PAIN. And that about does it. Now that you've got the hang of it, here's another cipher, based on a quote from Roger Bacon:

YEL HOOLOY TLJ NJG HCTLJ NUL JCH DSJCUNJY CP
TNJK YEDJSO HEDME YEL MCTTCJ MUCHG CP VLCVAL
HDAA BJGLUOYNJG DJ YEL PBYBUL**

It helps to know that the most common two-letter words in English are, in descending order, OF, TO, IN, IT, IS, HE, BY, OR, AS, AT, AN, and SO. The most common three-letter words are THE, AND, FOR, ARE, BUT, ALL, and NOT. The most-used four-letter words: THAT, WITH, FROM, HAVE, THIS, and THEY.

Notice that, in both cryptograms, I put the ciphertext in groups that are the same length as the plain-text words. If I'd run the letters all together, or printed them in groups of equal length, the cipher would be a lot harder to crack.

Excerpt from Arabic philosopher al-Kindi's treatise on cryptography, which influenced al-Qalqashandi's work.

** The wisest men and women are now ignorant of many things which the common crowd of people will understand in the future.

CHAPTER FOUR

A Disk, a Grille, and a Tableau

1412 CE – 1586 CE

Early in the fourteenth century, Italian philosophers and writers had begun looking longingly back to ancient Rome and Greece and trying to recapture what was regarded as a golden age of intellectual and artistic accomplishment. Ironically, in imitating the cultures of the past, the Italians laid the foundations of modern European art, philosophy, science, and political systems—and modern cryptology.

Many of Italy's independent city-states were ruled by powerful families—for example, the notorious Medicis of Florence. Under such wealthy patrons, the fine arts flourished. Unfortunately, so did the art of war, as the city-states competed for trade and territory.

Luckily, the art of diplomacy was developing, too. Each of the larger city-states sent ambassadors to negotiate with—and to spy on—their rivals. And according to author David

Medici coat of arms

Kahn, "The growth of cryptology resulted directly from the flowering of modern diplomacy."

Most ruling families had at least one secretary who could encipher secret communications. And if any secret dispatches from other city-states happened to fall into their masters' hands, the secretaries got to use their *deciphering* skills.

The old reliable monoalphabetic cipher was no longer so reliable, thanks to those Muslim scholars and their discovery of frequency analysis. By the early fifteenth century, secretive Italian nobles had begun using *homophonic* ciphers that provided several substitutes, or homophones, for the most common letters of the alphabet. Here's a system similar to one created for the duke of Mantua:

a	b	c	d	e	f	g	h	i	j	k	l	m	n	o	p	q	r	s	t	u	v	w	x	y	z
z	y	x	w	v	u	t	s	r	q	p	o	n	m	l	k	j	i	h	g	f	e	d	c	b	a
2				4				8					6						5						
5				7				3					9												

So an "e" might appear in the ciphertext as a **v**, a **4**, or a **7**. But a monoalphabetic cipher with homophones is still a monoalphabetic cipher, and it's still easy prey for an experienced cryptanalyst. Frustrated at having their messages read by their rivals, politicians searched for a more secure method of enciphering. Around 1466, Leon Battista Alberti of Florence provided one.

The term *Renaissance man* is used to describe someone who's well informed on a wide variety of subjects. If Leonardo da Vinci is the perfect model of the Renaissance man, Alberti runs a close second. He was, among other things, a painter, a composer and musician, a poet and essayist, a philosopher, and an architect. Ironically, one of the few skills he hadn't mastered was cryptography. But then Pope Paul II's personal secretary mentioned to Alberti that the pope could use a good, unbreakable cipher. Alberti promised to give the matter some thought.

He did a lot more than that. He penned a twenty-five-page essay that discussed most of the existing methods of cryptography and cryptanalysis, then introduced a method that Alberti claimed was "worthy of kings." This may sound immodest, but in fact he had discovered what modern author and code expert Simon Singh calls "the most significant breakthrough in encryption for over a thousand years"—the *polyalphabetic* cipher.

What's more, Alberti had invented the first practical, secure enciphering device—the cipher disk—which he describes this way:

> I *make two circles out of copper plates. One, the larger, is called stationary, the smaller is called movable. . . . I divide the cir-*

cumference of each circle into 24 equal parts. . . . In the various cells of the larger circle I write the capital letters.

The letters *K*, *W*, and *Y* aren't used in Italian, so Alberti omitted them; for some reason, he also left out *H* and *U*. In each cell of the smaller circle, he printed lowercase letters,

not in regular order like the stationary characters, but scattered at random. . . . After completing these arrangements we place the smaller circle upon the larger so that a needle driven through the centers of both may serve as the axis of both and the movable plate may be revolved around it.

The disk looked like this:

The outer ring contains the plaintext alphabet; the inner ring has the ciphertext alphabet. With the disk in this position, the

D GLVN, D JULOOH, DQG D WDEOHHDX

word AXIS is enciphered as **dkbq**. Just like a monoalphabetic cipher, so far.

But here's the big breakthrough: After enciphering several words, you turn the dial to a different position, which gives you a whole new cipher alphabet and a whole new ball game. After a couple more words, turn it again for a totally different alphabet. And so on, to the end of the message.

Apparently Alberti didn't consider his polyalphabetic cipher secure enough. He gave it an extra layer of complexity by adding the numbers 1 through 4. This lets the sender substitute numbers for important or frequently used words, creating a code list, or *nomenclator*. For example, the number **21** might represent the word "Florence"; **413** might be "the pope"; **3112** could be "Lorenzo de' Medici." To include these code numbers in a message, you encipher them, just as you did the plaintext letters; with the disk in the above position, 413 would be **rpm**.

Leon Battista
Alberti

Italian, 1404-1472,
Inventor of the
Alberti cipher disk.

The Renaissance Version of the Floppy Disk

If you want to see exactly how Alberti's cipher disk worked, you can make your own version. Photocopy the disks below, paste them on cardboard, and cut them out. Place the small disk on top of the larger one and stick a thumbtack or pushpin through the center. Naturally, anyone you send a message to needs a duplicate device.

Remember: Outer ring, plaintext; inner ring, ciphertext. For our trial run, let's use Alberti's own words as the plaintext: WORTHY OF KINGS.

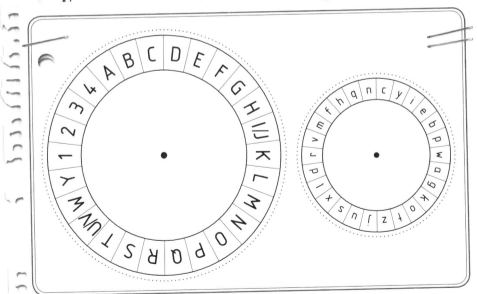

✂ Photocopy and cut out along dotted line

First, pick a letter on the inner ring to serve as your *cipher key*—let's say **x**. Turn it so the **x** lines up with any letter on the outer ring—let's say the A. Print a capital **A** as the first letter of your enciphered message. It's not actually part of the message; it just tells the receiver how to line up the disks.

Now print (in lower case) the cipher letters that appear under the plaintext letters W, O, R, T, H, and Y—**o e w g h t**, right? Time to change the alphabet. Line your key letter **x** up with a different plaintext letter—P, this time. Print a capital **P** in your ciphertext, then print the cipher letters that appear under O and F—**s** and **a**. Line up the **x** with something new—the Q. Print a capital Q in your ciphertext, then the letters that appear under K, I, N, G, and S—**o k j a d**. (For a plaintext letter X, use the number 1; for a plaintext Z, the number 2.)

Using frequency analysis on a polyalphabetic cipher like this is a waste of time. You can't tell how often a letter appears, because its ciphertext equivalent keeps changing. It's really tough to crack an Alberti cryptogram unless you have an

identical disk and you know what key letter the sender used, in which case you just
align the disk the same way the sender did
and write down the plaintext letters that
appear above the ciphertext letters.

Here's a cryptogram to solve, a quote
from fifteenth-century Italian writer
Niccolò Machiavelli. The key letter will
be x again:

Mdlk zpf hd wk Go shw df hcjuc Txt uictbowmi
xuqzs, Rcze c ogjz dj Ogrtkomas xgg hxjfav *

Since popes and kings and dictators were so anxious to find a
secure cipher, you might think they'd welcome Alberti's system
with open arms. But it took a while for the cipher disk to catch
on—about four centuries, in fact.

Most Renaissance cryptologists continued using variations
of the same old same old: substituting numbers for the plaintext letters, adding *nulls*—letters and symbols that have no
meaning—creating extensive and elaborate nomenclators, and
writing invisibly. Even so, it took a lot of skill to encipher and
decipher messages quickly and accurately. Venice established
a school for training new recruits and held regular cipher-
cracking contests. Cipher secretaries who made improvements to

D GLVN, D JULOOH, DQG D WDEOHDX

* One has to be a fox in order to recognize traps, and a lion to frighten off wolves.

the art were given bonuses. Those who revealed its secrets could be sentenced to death.

Around the turn of the sixteenth century, Alberti's concept of the polyalphabetic cipher was rediscovered by a German monk who called himself Johannes Trithe-

Johannes Trithemius
German, 1462–1516, author of Polygraphia

mius. Trithemius was a serious scholar whose contributions to the fields of history, biography, and bibliography were overshadowed by his fascination with such esoteric subjects as alchemy, astrology, and witchcraft.

In his 1499 work, *Steganographia*, Trithemius described several methods of secret writing that he claimed had been taught to him by a spirit, in a dream. Some were quite practical, such as hiding the message within groups of nulls so that it could be deciphered by reading every other letter of every other group. For example, **JHME VTTX ALRL POCQ GOG** would yield HELLO.

But he also claimed that if you wrapped up your message in a picture of the person you were sending it to, buried it under the threshold of the house, and said the proper incantation, it would be delivered telepathically by a network of angels. Talk about secure. The occult elements in *Steganographia* earned Trithemius a reputation as a practitioner of black magic.

In 1508, he penned a more down-to-earth work, *Polygraphia*, that introduced a crucial tool of modern cryptology, the *tableau*. It's simply a series of alphabets, one beneath the other, each shifted one place to the left, like this:

A B C D E F G H I J K L M N O P Q R S T U V W X Y Z
B C D E F G H I J K L M N O P Q R S T U V W X Y Z A
C D E F G H I J K L M N O P Q R S T U V W X Y Z A B
D E F G H I J K L M N O P Q R S T U V W X Y Z A B C

and so on, twenty-six times. The top line is the plaintext alphabet. To encipher the word MONK, start with line 1; M is enciphered as itself, **M**. Then go to line 2 and use the cipher letter beneath the plaintext letter O—**P**. Go to line 3 and print the letter beneath the plaintext N—**P** again. Go to line 4 and print the letter beneath the plaintext K—**N**. It's a lot like the Caesar cipher, except that you use a different alphabet to encipher each letter. If you know the sender is using a tableau, of course,

A copy of *Polygraphia* dating from 1518

D GLVN, D JI LOOH, DQG D WDEOHDX

it's easy to construct your own and do the above procedure in reverse.

Like Alberti's disk, Trithemius's tableau was largely ignored. In 1556, yet another Italian Renaissance man came up with a system that was actually used during his lifetime. Though Girolamo Cardano wrote some 240 books on such weighty subjects as mathematics, astronomy, physics, probability theory, music, and medicine, he wasn't your typical sober scholar; he was, in the words of modern author and scientist Isaac Asimov, "a thoroughgoing knave and rascal, a gambler, cheat, given to murderous rage, insufferably conceited."

Cardano's fame as a writer quickly faded, but the cipher device that bears his name is still used today. The Cardano grille is even simpler than Alberti's disk. It consists of a single piece of paper ruled off into thirty-six squares, with nine of the squares cut out. You place the grille on another sheet of paper and print a letter of the plaintext in each opening. Then you turn the grille and print nine more letters, and so on, leaving a grid of ciphertext on the paper underneath.

Girolamo Cardano

Italian, 1501–1576, creator of the Cardano Grille.

Cooking up Ciphers on a Cardano Grille

Like the scytale, the Cardano grille creates a transposition cipher; it uses the same letters as the plaintext but scrambles them. To make the grille, photocopy the figure below on a sheet of heavy paper and cut it out, then cut out all the white squares.

· CARDANO GRILLE ·

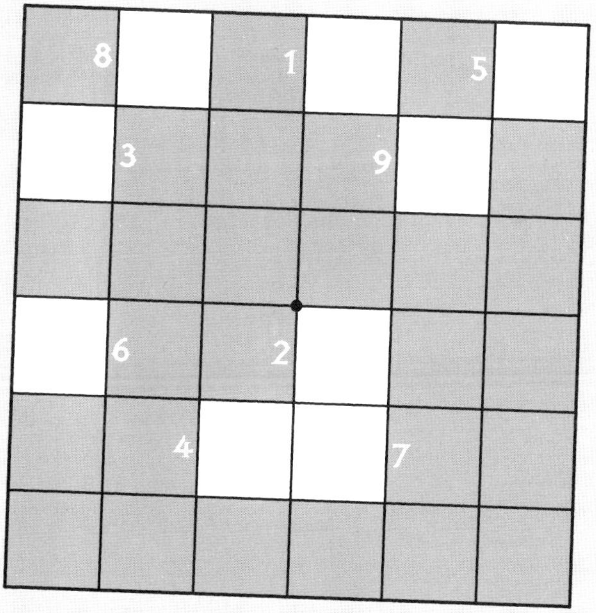

M
—
W

Lay the grille on a plain sheet of paper, stick a pushpin through the center, and you're ready to encipher any message up to thirty-six letters long. Try this quote from the sixteenth-century satirist Rabelais: THE APPETITE GROWS BY EATING. Print the first nine letters in the cut-out squares, starting with number one and going in numerical order.

Now turn the grille ninety degrees clockwise and print the next nine letters. Turn it another ninety degrees and finish the phrase. You'll have three empty spaces left, which you can fill with nulls, or random letters. In actual practice, you'd use some of the same letters that appear in your plaintext, so the cipher is harder to break. But for now, just use Xs. Turn another ninety degrees and fill the rest of the empty boxes with Xs.

Lift up the grille, and you should have a grid of ciphertext that looks like this:

```
X T W T G P
E X X I I B
X R A X X G
P S E H X T
X X A E Y T
N X E X X O
```

While most Italian cryptographers were using variations of the creaky old monoalphabetic cipher, French scholar Blaise de Vigenère (veeg-en-AIR) was studying the work of Alberti and Trithemius and developing what David Kahn calls "the archetypal system of polyalphabetic substitution and probably the most famous cipher system of all time."

In his 1586 book *Traicté des Chiffres*, Vigenère proposed what he called *le chiffre indéchiffrable*—the unbreakable cipher. It uses a tableau much like Trithemius's, but with some significant improvements, most importantly the use of a *key*.

Remember that Trithemius just started in the top row, moved down to the second, the third, and so on. The resulting cryptogram is easy to read if you make a tableau of your own. To create a really secure cipher, you need to mix up the order in which the alphabets are used. Vigenère has you choose a word or phrase as a key; the letters of the key indicate which row of the tableau to use next. The sidebar shows exactly how this works.

D GLVN, D JULOOH, DQG D WDEOHDX

The Pretty Secure but Not Unbreakable Cipher

To be perfectly fair to Vigenère, the cipher that follows is not the one he called *le chiffre indéchiffrable*. Though Vigenère put the version on page 43 in his book, he never claimed it was unbreakable. Nevertheless, cryptographers used it for centuries, believing it was totally secure. It isn't. But it is pretty secure. On page 43 is a modern rendering of the Vigenère tableau.

The lowercase letters on top are the plaintext letters. The CAPITALS IN ITALICS to the left of the tableau are the key letters. The **BOLD CAPITALS** are the ciphertext letters. For the plaintext, here's a quote from Vigenère's countryman, playwright Jean Racine: "Honor without money is just a disease." To encipher it, you need a keyword—let's say MONEY. Print it on top of the plaintext repeatedly, like this;

```
MONEYMONEYMONEYMONEYMONEYMONEYM
Honorwithoutmoneyisjustadisease
```

The letters of the keyword tell you which row of the tableau to use. Go to the

M row and run your finger along it until you reach the column with the plaintext letter "h" at the top. Your ciphertext letter is **T**. Next run your finger along the O alphabet until you get to the "o" column; write down an **C**. The "n" column of the N alphabet gives you the ciphertext letter **A**. And so on. You should end up with this for a ciphertext:

TCASPIWGLMGHZSLQMVWHGGGEBUGREQQ

Frequency analysis won't help decipher it; as with the Alberti disk, a plaintext letter is seldom enciphered the same way twice. It's a tough system to crack, and as Vigenère pointed out, "the longer the key is, the more difficult it is to solve the cipher."

When you're going to send a secret message, you give your friend the keyword in advance. To read it, all he or she has to do is print the keyword repeatedly on top of the ciphertext, then consult the tableau, which shows that, in the M alphabet, the **T** appears in the column under the plaintext letter "h."

As you'll discover, it is possible to break this cipher without the keyword. But for now, let's see what Vigenère really had in mind for his chiffre indéchiffrable.

He proposed using the plaintext itself as

D GLVN, D JULOOH, DQG D WDEOHDX

the key—a technique known today as an autokey. Here's how it works. First you need a
secret *primer key*, a single letter that you
reveal only to the receiver; lets say it's
a Q. Print a Q above the first letter of the
plaintext. Then, above the rest of the letters, print the *plaintext itself*:

Q H O N O R W I T H O U T M O N E Y I S J U S T A D I S E A S
H o n o r w i t h o u t m o n e y i s j u s t a d i s e a s e

Use the Q alphabet to turn the plaintext
H into a ciphertext **X**. Use the "H" alphabet
to make the "o" into a **V**, and so on. In
effect, you're using a keyword as long
as the message itself, so it never repeats.
And, as you'll discover, a repeating
keyword is the fatal flaw of the Pretty
Secure but Not Unbreakable version of the
Vigenère cipher—which, unfortunately, is
the version that got passed down through
history.

For your edification and entertain-
ment, here's a line from French playwright
Molière, enciphered using the Pretty
Secure method and the keyword *MONEY*:

ABR HGQG BRJK CAGC MBQ MRE TBV QGQU E JABT
XGYS*

* One dies only once, and it's for such a long time.

The Vigenère Tableau

	a	b	c	d	e	f	g	h	i	j	k	l	m	n	o	p	q	r	s	t	u	v	w	x	y	z
A	A	B	C	D	E	F	G	H	I	J	K	L	M	N	O	P	Q	R	S	T	U	V	W	X	Y	Z
B	B	C	D	E	F	G	H	I	J	K	L	M	N	O	P	Q	R	S	T	U	V	W	X	Y	Z	A
C	C	D	E	F	G	H	I	J	K	L	M	N	O	P	Q	R	S	T	U	V	W	X	Y	Z	A	B
D	D	E	F	G	H	I	J	K	L	M	N	O	P	Q	R	S	T	U	V	W	X	Y	Z	A	B	C
E	E	F	G	H	I	J	K	L	M	N	O	P	Q	R	S	T	U	V	W	X	Y	Z	A	B	C	D
F	F	G	H	I	J	K	L	M	N	O	P	Q	R	S	T	U	V	W	X	Y	Z	A	B	C	D	E
G	G	H	I	J	K	L	M	N	O	P	Q	R	S	T	U	V	W	X	Y	Z	A	B	C	D	E	F
H	H	I	J	K	L	M	N	O	P	Q	R	S	T	U	V	W	X	Y	Z	A	B	C	D	E	F	G
I	I	J	K	L	M	N	O	P	Q	R	S	T	U	V	W	X	Y	Z	A	B	C	D	E	F	G	H
J	J	K	L	M	N	O	P	Q	R	S	T	U	V	W	X	Y	Z	A	B	C	D	E	F	G	H	I
K	K	L	M	N	O	P	Q	R	S	T	U	V	W	X	Y	Z	A	B	C	D	E	F	G	H	I	J
L	L	M	N	O	P	Q	R	S	T	U	V	W	X	Y	Z	A	B	C	D	E	F	G	H	I	J	K
M	M	N	O	P	Q	R	S	T	U	V	W	X	Y	Z	A	B	C	D	E	F	G	H	I	J	K	L
N	N	O	P	Q	R	S	T	U	V	W	X	Y	Z	A	B	C	D	E	F	G	H	I	J	K	L	M
O	O	P	Q	R	S	T	U	V	W	X	Y	Z	A	B	C	D	E	F	G	H	I	J	K	L	M	N
P	P	Q	R	S	T	U	V	W	X	Y	Z	A	B	C	D	E	F	G	H	I	J	K	L	M	N	O
Q	Q	R	S	T	U	V	W	X	Y	Z	A	B	C	D	E	F	G	H	I	J	K	L	M	N	O	P
R	R	S	T	U	V	W	X	Y	Z	A	B	C	D	E	F	G	H	I	J	K	L	M	N	O	P	Q
S	S	T	U	V	W	X	Y	Z	A	B	C	D	E	F	G	H	I	J	K	L	M	N	O	P	Q	R
T	T	U	V	W	X	Y	Z	A	B	C	D	E	F	G	H	I	J	K	L	M	N	O	P	Q	R	S
U	U	V	W	X	Y	Z	A	B	C	D	E	F	G	H	I	J	K	L	M	N	O	P	Q	R	S	T
V	V	W	X	Y	Z	A	B	C	D	E	F	G	H	I	J	K	L	M	N	O	P	Q	R	S	T	U
W	W	X	Y	Z	A	B	C	D	E	F	G	H	I	J	K	L	M	N	O	P	Q	R	S	T	U	V
X	X	Y	Z	A	B	C	D	E	F	G	H	I	J	K	L	M	N	O	P	Q	R	S	T	U	V	W
Y	Y	Z	A	B	C	D	E	F	G	H	I	J	K	L	M	N	O	P	Q	R	S	T	U	V	W	X
Z	Z	A	B	C	D	E	F	G	H	I	J	K	L	M	N	O	P	Q	R	S	T	U	V	W	X	Y

D GLVN, D JULOOH, DQG D WDEOHDX

Though Vigenère didn't originate the idea of the tableau, his name has become forever attached to it. He wasn't the first to suggest using a keyword, either; that honor goes to an obscure Italian scholar named Belaso. What Vigenère *did* do was take the ideas of others and synthesize them into a system that was head and shoulders above anything else in use at the time, a system that forms the basis of many modern ciphers. One of Vigenère's contemporaries declared, "The key cipher is the noblest and the greatest in the world, the most secure and faithful that never was there man who could find it out."

That claim would prove to be a bit of an exaggeration.

Blaise de
Vigenère
French, 1523–1596
creator of the
Unbreakable Cipher

CHAPTER FIVE

Babington, Beer, and Baconian Biliteralism

1586 CE – 1603 CE

Queen Elizabeth I
English, 1533–1603, queen of England and Ireland from 1558–1603

Since the British Isles are isolated by the sea from the rest of Europe, it always took a while for new ideas and fashions from the Continent to make their way to England. But under Queen Elizabeth I, who took the throne in 1558, the country underwent an artistic and philosophical renaissance to rival Italy's. Britain was also in the throes of a religious upheaval; the old faith, Catholicism, was being replaced by Protestantism. Like the Renaisssance, the Protestant Reformation started in continental Europe; Elizabeth's father, Henry VIII, introduced it to England, and his daughter embraced the new religion.

The more radical and resentful Catholics were continually

Mary Stuart
Scottish, 1542–1587,
queen of Scotland
and disputed heir
to English throne

plotting to get rid of Elizabeth. As a defense, the queen created a network of spies and informers, headed by her principal secretary, Francis Walsingham.

During the reign of the Catholic Queen Mary I (1553–1558), Walsingham fled to Europe, where he studied the latest cryptographic developments, including Cardano's grille. When Elizabeth took the throne in 1558, Walsingham returned to England and established a spy school to teach these methods.

Its most celebrated pupil was the playwright Christopher Marlowe, whose murder at the age of twenty-nine was probably linked to his work as a secret agent. Cryptologically speaking, though, the school's most distinguished graduate was Thomas Phelippes, England's first great codebreaker.

Phelippes had a working knowledge of all the major European languages and was a master of frequency analysis. He spent most of his time deciphering the secret communications of foreign ambassadors. Then, in 1586, he got the biggest cryptological challenge of his career.

At that time the Catholic church recognized Mary Stuart—

queen of Scotland and granddaughter of Henry VIII's sister—as the rightful ruler of England. For nineteen years, Queen Elizabeth had been keeping her kinswoman a virtual prisoner, fearing that Mary would lead a rebellion against her.

One of Mary's most fervent supporters was Anthony Babington, a rich young gentleman. In March 1586, Babington hatched a scheme to free Mary and assassinate Elizabeth. Using a combination cipher and nomenclator, Babington wrote to Mary:

> *Myself with ten gentlemen and a hundred of our followers will undertake the delivery of your royal person from the hands of your enemies. For the dispatch of the usurper [Elizabeth] . . . there be six noble gentlemen, all my private friends, who for the zeal they bear to the Catholic cause and your Majesty's service will undertake that tragical execution.*

Portion of the letter written by Anthony Babington to Mary Queen of Scots in his cipher/nomenclator.

The task of delivering the message to the closely guarded Queen of Scots fell to Gilbert Gifford, a supposedly staunch Catholic who once trained as a priest. Gifford devised a clever steganographic ploy: He sealed the paper inside a watertight packet and inserted it in a keg of beer bound for the country home where Mary was being held.

Gilbert Gifford's Secret Beer Keg

Message hidden inside hollow keg bung (cut-away view shown here)

False bottom screws into place (this end placed inside the keg)

Secret bung then used to seal beer keg

In reality, Gifford was a double agent. He turned a copy of the ciphertext over to spymaster Francis Walsingham, whose cryptanalyst, Phelippes, easily deciphered it. Instead of arresting Babington, Walsingham waited to see how Mary would reply to the proposal.

Mary was no stranger to the art of cryptography. She had made invisible ink by dissolving alum (a white or colorless mineral salt) in water, and suggested that correspondents conceal messages in books by "writing always on the fourth, eighth, twelfth and sixteenth leaf, and so on . . . and cause green ribbons to be attached to all the books that you've had written in this way." Yet she foolishly enciphered her reply in the same simple code Babington had used and sent it to him via Gifford's beer keg. The plaintext read, in part:

The affairs being thus prepared and forces in readiness both without and within the realm, then shall it be time to set the six gentlemen to work taking order, upon the accomplishing of their design.

The Queen of Scots was tried, found guilty largely on the basis of the deciphered message, and beheaded. Babington and his coconspirators were, according to a historian of the time, "bowelled alive and seeing, and quartered."

There's a lesson to be learned from their tragic fate: In the words of author Simon Singh, "A weak encryption can be worse than no encryption at all." Since Mary and Babington believed the cipher was secure, they discussed their plans more openly than they would have if they'd suspected their messages might be read.

Here's a sampling of the cipher/nomenclator that betrayed them:

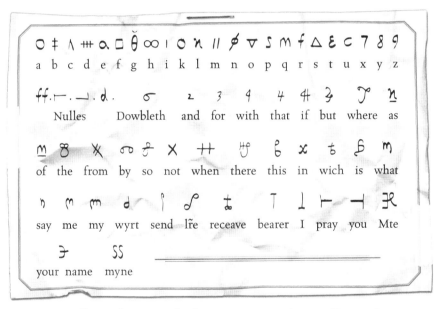

Ironically, only a year before Mary sent her sadly inadequate cipher message, Blaise de Vigenère had introduced his *chiffre indéchiffrable*. If Mary had used Vigenère's method, or even the Pretty Secure version, she might well have outwitted Walsingham and Phelippes.

But, despite its obvious superiority, Vigenère's tableau was largely ignored, even scorned, for most of the sixteenth and seventeenth centuries. Though it found favor with a few hard-core cryptography enthusiasts, most considered it too troublesome. And they had a point.

As Vigenère himself admitted, it is "somewhat tedious to encipher long texts using such a table." Even worse, if the sender makes a single mistake, such as omitting one letter in one repetition of the keyword, it scrambles the rest of the message so badly that, as a nineteenth-century cryptologist put it, "the confederate with his key shall never set it in order again."

Most military leaders and heads of state preferred a quicker, simpler method of communicating in secret, such as a *nomenclator*—a list of commonly used words, each with a code number—or a combination of substitution cipher and nomenclator. As the popularity of nomenclators grew, so did the nomenclators themselves, until diplomats were lugging around massive volumes containing several thousand words or phrases and their equivalent code numbers.

Nomenclators had other drawbacks, too. First, they could be stolen, making the code essentially worthless. Second, for the convenience of the sender and the receiver, plaintext words were usually listed alphabetically, then assigned code numbers that were in numerical order. Unfortunately, it was also convenient for anyone trying to break the code.

An oversimplified example: Suppose you deduce, from the structure of the message, that the number **214** stands for "the" and **216** means "there." You can reasonably assume that **215** is also a "th" word—probably "then." You've begun to crack the code.

In the mid-sixteenth century, Antoine Rossignol, cryptologist for the French king Louis XIV, solved this particular problem. He created a nomenclator that became known as *Le Grand Chiffre*—the Great Cipher. (According to the modern definition, of course, it was a code, not a cipher.)

It consisted of two parts: the *table à chiffrer* and the *table à déchiffrer*. The enciphering table listed the plaintext words alphabetically, so the sender could locate them easily, but the code numbers were assigned in random order. In the deciphering table, the code numbers were listed numerically, but the plaintext words weren't remotely alphabetical.

Antoine
Rossignol
French, 1600–
1682, creator
of le Grande
Ciffre.

Rossignol made the Great Cipher even greater by assigning the code numbers not to entire words but to syllables and individual letters; for example, the phrase *les ennemis* was broken up this way—*les en ne mi s*—and enciphered as **124 22 125 46 345**. The code was so secure that it baffled cryptanalysts for the next two hundred years.

Though nomenclators remained popular well into the eighteenth century, a few dedicated cryptographers went on experimenting, searching for the perfect system—easy to use and hard to steal or solve.

After Queen Elizabeth died in 1603, the throne of England passed to James, son of Mary, Queen of Scots. Mary would not have been pleased, for James was a Protestant. He appointed as his lord chancellor Sir Francis Bacon, a lawyer, scientist, and philosopher. Bacon devised a new form of cryptography that combined enciphering and steganography.

Bacon's *biliteral cipher* was the direct ancestor of Morse code and of the binary system used in today's computers. But instead of dots and dashes or ones and zeroes, Bacon used **A**s and **B**s. His biliteral alphabet looked like this:

a **AAAAA**	e **AABAA**	i/j **ABAAA**	n **ABBAA**	r **BAAAA**	w **BABAA**
b **AAAAB**	f **AABAB**	k **ABAAB**	o **ABBAB**	s **BAAAB**	x **BABAB**
c **AAABA**	g **AABBA**	l **ABABA**	p **ABBBA**	t **BAABA**	y **BABBA**
d **AAABB**	h **AABBB**	m **ABABB**	q **ABBBB**	u/v **BAABB**	z **BABBB**

So if you use the system as an ordinary cipher, the word "Bacon" is enciphered: **AAAAB AAAAA AAABA ABBAB ABBAA**.

In this form, it's just another substitution cipher. But for added security, the ciphertext can be concealed within another, seemingly innocuous, message. If you want to know exactly how . . . you guessed it: Check out the sidebar.

M SIDEBAR W

Writing Anything by Anything

With his method, Bacon said, a person could write *omnia per omnia*, or anything by anything. In other words, you can write down any sequence of words and, by using a clever steganographic technique, convey a hidden message to the receiver.

This part of the process uses biliteralism, too. You have to write the letters of your message in two distinct styles. To show you how it works, I'll use two different type styles.

For simplicity, let's use a one-word plaintext: "HELP." Since you need five cipher letters for each plaintext letter, the ciphertext has to be at least five times as long. We'll use a quote from Sir Francis: **KNOWLEDGE ITSELF IS POWER.**

First, divide the ciphertext into five-letter groups; put one letter of the plaintext above each group. Then consult Bacon's biliteral cipher and print the cipher equivalent of each plaintext letter right beneath it, so you have:

```
    H        E        L        P
  AABBB   AABAA   ABABA   ABBBA
  KNOWL   EDGEI   TSELF   ISPOW  ER
```

To put the ciphertext in its final form, print the cipher letters beneath the As in one script and the letters beneath the Bs in a different one. I'll use ordinary type for the A script and italics for the B script. (The last two letters are nulls, so it doesn't matter which typeface I use):

KNOWLEDGE *ITSELF* IS *POWER*

To decipher the cryptogram, divide it into five-letter groups, convert the ordinary letters into As and the italics into Bs, and then find the plaintext letters by consulting the biliteral alphabet. Bacon's system is even more time-consuming and error-prone than Vigenère's, so you certainly wouldn't want to send a very long message with it.

Sir Francis
Bacon

English, 1561–1626,
Creator of the
Biliteral Cipher.

CHAPTER SIX

Prisons, Pigpens, and Black Chambers

—————— 1603 CE – 1775 CE ——————

King Charles I

English, 1600–1649, king of England, Scotland and Ireland

F rancis Bacon's patron, James I, was continu- ally at odds with the Eng- lish Parliament, which felt it should have a bigger role in running the country. After James's death, his son, Charles I, inherited both the throne and the dispute with Parliament—which, in 1642, turned into a full-fledged civil war. If cryptology flourishes in an age of diplomacy, in a time of war it is put to the ultimate test; like the strength of a sword arm, the strength of a code or cipher can mean the difference between life and death.

For Sir John Trevanion, it meant life. Trevanion, who fought for the king, was captured by the forces of Parliament—known as Roundheads—and imprisoned in Colchester Castle. As he awaited execution, he received this innocent-looking message:

Worthie Sir John: Hope, that is the beste comfort of the af-
flicted, cannot much, I fear me, help you now. That I would
saye to you, is this only: if ever I may be able to requite that I
do owe you, stand not upon asking me. 'Tis not much I can do:
but what I can do, bee you verie sure I wille. I knowe that, if
deathe comes, if ordinary men fear it, it frights not you, ac-
counting it for a high honour, to have such a rewarde of your
loyalty. Pray yet that you may be spared this soe bitter, cup. I
fear not that you will grudge any sufferings; onlie if bie sub-
mission you can turn them away, 'tis the part of a wise man.
Tell me, an if you can, to do for you anythinge that you wolde
have done. The general goes back on Wednesday. Restinge your
servant to command. R. T.

Sir John asked for some time alone in the chapel to pray. When he failed to come out, the guards burst in to find their prisoner gone. If the Roundheads had been as clever as Sir John, they'd have realized that the seemingly harmless note actually contained instructions on how to escape.

"R.T.'s" cipher is basically the same one Trithemius discussed

Sir John
Wallis

English,
1616–1703,
mathematician and
cryptographer

briefly in his book *Steg-anographia*. It's called a *null cipher*, and as you may recall (or not), it conceals the letters of the plaintext within a string of other letters. While Trithemius used meaningless groups of letters, Sir John's friend used sensible—if rather awkward—sentences. To unmask the message within the message, print the third letter after each punctuation mark. *

Sir John was more fortunate than his king. Like his grandmother, Mary Queen of Scots, Charles I was betrayed by a cipher that was too easily broken.

To bring down the king, the leader of the Roundheads, Oliver Cromwell, needed to prove him guilty of plotting against Parliament. In June 1645, Cromwell got the proof he required. The Roundheads intercepted a number of Royalist military dispatches and presented them to Cromwell's cipher secretary, Sir John Wallis, a mathematician and clergyman.

Among the dispatches Wallis found several enciphered letters written by King Charles to his queen. When deciphered, the messages showed that the king was directly involved in attempts to destroy Parliament. After the Royalists were defeated,

* Panel at east end of chapel slides

Charles was tried and, thanks partly to the incriminating letters, found guilty of treason. He was beheaded in 1649.

Several decades after Charles's insecure cipher cost him his life, a French soldier known as the chevalier de Rohan was the victim of a cipher that was *too* secure. During the Third Anglo-Dutch War (1672–1674), in which France and England were allies, Rohan and an accomplice named Trouaumont were imprisoned for giving military secrets to the enemy.

Trouaumont was taken away to be interrogated. Rohan feared that his friend, who was near death, would confess. Before Rohan himself was questioned, he received a bundle of clothing and, hidden within it, this message:

mg eulhxcclgw ghj yxuj lm ct ulgc alj

When the guards came to fetch him, the chevalier was still struggling with the ciphertext. Believing that Trouaumont had confessed already, Rohan broke down and told all and was sentenced to death.

He might have saved himself, if only he'd deciphered that message. It's a simple substitution cipher, easily solved (provided you're familiar with French) by using frequency analysis. **Mg** is most likely the common French article, *le*, meaning "the." And if all the **g**s are "e"s, then **ghj** is probably the frequently used verb *est*, meaning "is." If you continue in that vein, you get *Le prison-nier est mort; il n'a rien dit*—"The prisoner [Trouaumont] is dead; he said nothing."

By the early eighteenth century, the art of cryptography was being discovered by other organizations with secrets to keep, including two fraternal societies, the Rosicrucians and the Freemasons. To guard their rituals and their business affairs, both organizations used variations of the *pigpen cipher,* or *tic-tac-toe cipher.*

Though the ciphertext it creates looks daunting, the pigpen system is really just a simple substitution cipher. The Rosicrucians' version is based on a grid like this one:

a b c	d e f	g h i
j k l	m n o	p q r
s t u	v w x	y z

To create a ciphertext letter, draw one of the nine sections of the grid and put a dot inside it that indicates the position of the plaintext letter. So, a plaintext "a" is enciphered as ⌟. A "q" becomes ⌐, an "x" is ⌐, and so on. Here's a pigpen cryptogram to solve, based on a quote from French philosopher and mathematician (and Rosicrucian) René Descartes:

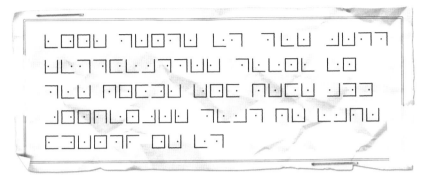

While the Renaissance was making its way through Europe and England, Russia had remained comparatively isolated. Around the middle of the seventeenth century, the country finally opened itself up to trade and diplomacy with the West. And as always, the development of diplomacy led to a need for secret communications.

Peter I (Peter the Great), who ruled from 1682 to 1725, was the first czar to travel outside of Russia. During visits to Holland, England, and France, he undoubtedly saw Western cryptologists in action. Soon Russian diplomats were using codes and ciphers of their own.

Their first efforts were predictably simple—mostly monoalphabetic ciphers with invented symbols. But by the reign of Peter's daughter Elizabeth (1741–1761), Russian cryptographers had developed a two-part nomenclator that contained 3,500

M/W

Peter the Great
Russian, 1672–1725,
emperor of Russia

code words and used nulls and homophones (more than one code number for each word).

As an extra precaution, senders sometimes wrote in invisible ink between the lines of a mundane message. "Not having at hand the sympathetic ink that I have been using," wrote the foreign minister to one of his ambassadors, "I used lemon juice today in the attached confidential letter; consequently, instead of dipping it into aqua fortis [nitric acid], it must be heated."

By the late 1700s, Russia had not only caught up cryptologically with its European neighbors but had surpassed many of them. Like most major powers, Russia was no longer content with just a cipher secretary or two; it established what the French called a *cabinet noir*, or black chamber—a government-sanctioned team of skilled forgers, translators, and cryptanalysts who intercepted and opened foreign dispatches, read or deciphered them, then sent them on their way. Ideally, the receiver never realized his mail had been tampered with.

The French ambassador to Russia, the marquis de la Chétardie, knew his mail was being examined by the Russian Black Chamber, but assumed that its cryptanalysts were too inept to crack his cipher. He was wrong. The marquis had penned some unkind remarks about the empress Elizabeth, calling her, among other things, "frivolous" and "dissipated." She promptly banished him from Russia.

Probably the most efficient Black Chamber in Europe was Austria's ten-man *Geheime Kabinets-Kanzlei*. Its translators could read nearly any European language, including Armenian. Its clerks could melt the wax seal on a letter, copy the contents in shorthand, then expertly reseal it with a forged seal, all in a matter of minutes.

Codebreakers were becoming so sophisticated that monoalphabetic ciphers didn't stand a chance; senders were forced to switch to the more cumbersome polyalphabetic methods. At last Vigenère's system started getting the recognition it deserved, even if it was only the Pretty Secure version.

England's Black Chamber, called the Decyphering Branch, was probably the only such organization to be run by a bishop. When Edward Wiles became senior decypherer in 1716, he was a twenty-two-year-old minister. Though the church kept promoting Wiles, finally making him bishop of St. David's, he stayed in charge of the Decyphering Branch until his death in 1773. He even hired three of his sons as decypherers, making the Branch into something of a family enterprise. Eventually, three of his grandsons would also work for the organization.

The Branch's cryptanalysts were considered especially clever. But a French diplomat claimed that they "owe the Esteem they have gain'd solely to the negligence of those who give bad Cyphers, and to that of Ministers and their Secretaries, who make not a right use of them."

Though England had become as cryptologically savvy as the rest of Europe, that knowledge hadn't yet made its way to England's American Colonies. Like Russia, America had to develop the art of diplomacy before it felt the need for codes and ciphers. And those codes and ciphers wouldn't be tested and perfected until the Colonies went to war.

The bishop's palace at St. David's cathedral, where Edward Wiles lived.

CHAPTER SEVEN

The Two Revolutions

—— 1775 CE – 1830 CE ——

The Americans got their first taste of British cryptography just before the Revolutionary War. In August 1775, a Rhode Island baker was asked to deliver a cryptogram to the British; instead he delivered it to General Washington. The

Nathan Hale
American, 1755-1776,
officer in the
Continental Army

monoalphabetic cipher used Greek letters and other odd symbols. Elbridge Gerry, a future vice president of the United States, helped decipher the message, using frequency analysis.

It proved to be an intelligence report sent by Washington's own general of hospitals, Dr. Benjamin Church, who was secretly working for the British. It revealed the locations and strength of American troops and artillery. For his treachery, Church was exiled to the West Indies, but the ship he sailed on was lost at sea.

The first cipher-related casualty on the American side was Nathan Hale, a former schoolteacher who had volunteered to spy for the Continental Army. In September 1776, Hale infiltrated British forces on Long Island, New York. Unfamiliar with codes, ciphers, or steganography, he wrote his reports in Latin and hid them in the soles of his shoes.

On his way back to the American lines, he was captured and searched. British officers had no trouble reading his Latin notes. Without benefit of a trial, Hale was found guilty of espionage and hanged from the limb of an apple tree. He was twenty-one years old.

A month after Hale's death, the Continental Congress sent seventy-year-old Ben Franklin across the Atlantic to try to talk

Benjamin Franklin

American, 1706–1790, author, diplomat, inventor, scientist

France into joining the American cause. During the seven years he spent in Europe, Franklin sent and received innumerable secret dispatches. With the British navy preying on American ships, about half of the United States' foreign correspondence ended up in enemy hands, so Franklin needed a really secure cipher.

He settled on a system devised by Charles Dumas, a classical scholar serving as an American agent in the Netherlands. As a key, Dumas and his correspondents used a long passage from a French essay. They numbered each letter and punctuation mark and used the numbers as their ciphertext. The first sentence of the key looks like this:

Using just this brief section of the key, a *v* can be enciphered either by a **1** or an **8**, and an *e* by a **5**, a **13**, a **24**, a **26**, or a **29**. Franklin got a bit lackadaisical in his use of the cipher, sticking mainly with the first hundred numbers, instead of jumping around at random, and enciphering only the most important words of the message. Still, the system worked well. Which is more than can be said for one devised by another American, James Lovell.

Lovell was a teacher, orator, delegate to the Continental Congress, and amateur cryptologist. He proposed a variation of the Vigenère tableau. Take a look at the version that appeared on page forty-three. In place of the column of letters on the far left,

Lovell put numbers. He also used a code word as the key. Suppose you want to encipher the word "hi" and the keyword is **go**. Run your finger down the "g" column until you reach the letter **H**; that's the second row, so you encipher the "h" as **2**. Go down the "o" column until you reach the **I**; that's the twenty-first row, so the "e" is enciphered as **21**.

Though Lovell's system seems pretty straightforward, the cryptograms he sent to John Adams totally baffled the future president. If Lovell revealed the keyword in a letter, he risked having it intercepted by the enemy. Instead he gave Adams clues that were themselves baffling. One key was the second and third letters of "the maiden Name of the Wife of that Gentleman from whom I sent you a Little Money on a Lottery Score." Another was the name of a family Lovell and Adams had visited. Adams replied peevishly:

> I know very well the name of the family where I spent the Evening . . . and have made my alphabet accordingly; but I am on this occasion, as on all others hitherto, unable to comprehend the sense of the passages in cypher.

Abigail Adams complained to Lovell that her husband "is no[t] adept in investigating ciphers and hates to be puzzeld [sic] for a meaning." When Lovell asked her to help John master the system, she replied, "I hate a cipher of any kind and have been so much more used to deal in realities with those I love, that I should make a miserable proficiency in modes and figures." Nevertheless, she made

M
W

John Adams
American, 1735-1826, second President of the United States

an effort and proved much more adept than John.

Though Lovell's cipher was a failure, his code-breaking skills helped win the Revolution. In the fall of 1781, the Continental Army had General Cornwallis and his troops surrounded at Yorktown, Virginia. The Americans seized a secret dispatch from the British commander Sir Henry Clinton and gave it to Lovell to decipher. The message was written in three different ciphers, and it took Lovell two days to break it, but the result was worth the effort. The dispatch said that the reinforcements Clinton had promised Cornwallis would be late. Armed with this knowledge, the Americans kept up their siege; five days later, Cornwallis surrendered.

Most American generals and diplomats of the time distrusted ciphers. They preferred nomenclators or invisible ink. George Washington imported a special ink—or "stain," as he called it—

from London. The general customarily put his secret messages between the lines of a phony text written in regular ink, but some of his spies wrote on an otherwise blank sheet, then hid it inside a sheaf of ordinary paper.

Benjamin Tallmadge, director of Washington's secret service, compiled a 763-word nomenclator of frequently used words and names but committed the classic error of listing the words alphabetically and the code numbers numerically. It was easy to guess that the number **711**, which was near the end of the list of numbers, stood for "Washington," which was near the end of the alphabet.

Tallmadge's network of spies, known as the Culper Ring, used a system that proved more secure than his nomenclator; the British never did figure out how it worked. Robert Townsend (code name: Samuel Culper Sr.) eavesdropped on British officers who were quartered at his house on Oyster Bay, Long Island. He sent the information via a courier in a small boat to his confederate, Abraham Woodhull (Samuel Culper Jr.), who passed it on to Tallmadge. Culper Sr. had a neighbor

George Washington
American, 1732–1799, commander-in-chief of the Continental Army, first President of the United States

hang petticoats and handkerchiefs on her clothesline in a particular order, a visual code that told Culper Jr.—who was across the bay, peering through a telescope—where to meet the courier.

Cover of William Blackstone's Commentaries on the Laws of England

• • • • — — • • — — • — • •

The Americans didn't come up with a two-part nomenclator until 1781. In the meantime, conscientious crytographers used a more time-consuming method—the *book code*.

Future chief justice John Jay, then foreign minister to Spain, used a French dictionary as his key. He located the plaintext word in the dictionary, then wrote down what page it was on, which column it appeared in, and in what line. It was a simple (but slow) matter for the receiver to find the word in an identical dictionary.

Benedict Arnold, whose name has become synonymous with the word *traitor*, employed a book code for more nefarious purposes. Arnold was one of Washington's most courageous and respected officers, but when less deserving men were promoted ahead of him, Arnold grew bitter. His resentment, plus a desperate need for money to pay debts, led him to sell out to the British.

He contacted a British officer, Major John André, and of-

WKH WZR UHYROXWLRQV

Benedict Arnold

American, 1741–1801
This Revolutionary War general switched sides to join the British and became a famous traitor.

fered to surrender the fort at West Point for the princely sum of $30,000. André, who fancied himself an accomplished spy and cryptographer, insisted on corresponding in book code, with Blackstone's *Commentaries on the Laws of England* as a key. "Three Numbers make a Word," André wrote, "the 1st is the Page the 2d the Line the third the Word." Unfortunately, many of the necessary plaintext words didn't appear in the *Commentaries* and had to be spelled out, letter by letter.

The impatient Arnold demanded that they use a different book. They settled on the *Universal Etymological English Dictionary*. Before the new system could be tested, their conspiracy was discovered.

André was lodging at the home of Robert Townsend (Culper Sr.); the letters from Arnold aroused the suspicions of Townsend's sister, who alerted Washington's spymaster. When André was captured, hidden in his boots were papers revealing the details of the conspiracy. He was hanged by the Americans as a spy. Arnold escaped and joined the enemy, but was always regarded with disdain by British officers and London society.

Nearly all the founding fathers found cryptography a useful tool, but the only one who relished it as an art was that post-Renaissance Renaissance man, Thomas Jefferson. In the 1780s, as America's ambassador to France, he tried Lovell's system, which had so frustrated John Adams. Jefferson couldn't master it, either. He had little more luck with a cipher used by future president James Monroe. To one of Monroe's cryptic messages, Jefferson replied:

What was my mortification when I came to apply the cypher to it to find that I could not make out one syllable . . . Whether you have taken up a cypher established with some other person, or whether it is from my own stupidity . . . I cannot tell.

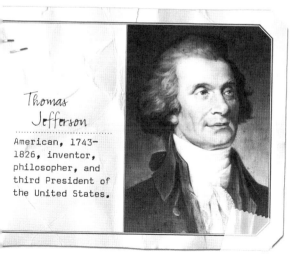

Thomas Jefferson

American, 1743–1826, inventor, philosopher, and third President of the United States.

But Jefferson was not nearly as clueless about codes and ciphers as these anecdotes make him seem. In fact, he invented a clever cyptological device he called a "wheel cypher." Like Alberti's disk, it was far ahead of its time; more

WKH WZR UHYROXWLRQV

than a century would pass before anyone really recognized its value. For a detailed description of the wheel cypher, see the sidebar.

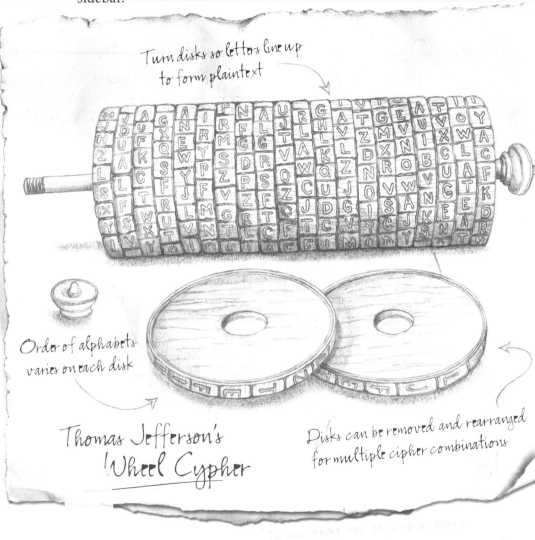

Turn disks so letters line up to form plaintext

Order of alphabets varies on each disk

Thomas Jefferson's Wheel Cypher

Disks can be removed and rearranged for multiple cipher combinations

Reinventing the Wheel Cipher

You can construct a crude version of Jefferson's wheel cypher from a sheet of thick foam-core poster board. With a compass, draw and cut out a bunch of two-inch circles—as many as you want; if you make thirty-six, as Jefferson recommends, you have a lot more patience than I do. With a gel pen or a fine-tip marker, print the letters of the alphabet in any order around the circumference of each disk. To get the spacing right, place each foam disk in the center of the Alberti disk illustrated on page thirty-one and mark off twenty-six segments.

Make a hole in the exact center of each disk with a hole punch. Slide the disks onto a pen or pencil, and you're ready to roll. The device works much the same way as a cylindrical bike lock whose numbers have to be lined up in the right order before it will open. Turn the disks on the wheel cypher so one row of letters spells out your plaintext. Then rotate the whole thing and write down the letters in one of the other twenty-five rows. That's your cipher-

WKH WZR UHYROXWLRQV

text. A friend with an identical wheel cypher just lines up the letters so they spell out the ciphertext, then turns the device until he or she spots a row of words that make sense.

Jefferson's gadget has one especially ingenious feature: the disks (which are numbered) can be arranged on the spindle in any order. So even if your wheel cypher is stolen, the culprit can't make out your message unless the disks are in the right sequence—and thirty-six disks can be arranged in 371, 993,326,789,901,217,467,999,448,150,835, 200,000,000 possible ways.

In 1922, the U.S. Army adopted a device almost identical to the wheel cypher. During World War II, the Germans and Japanese used the same elements Jefferson used—the disks, the jumbled alphabets, the changeable sequence—to create machines that stymied Allied codebreakers for years.

A number of foreigners fought for the American cause, including France's marquis de Lafayette and Count Axel Fersen of Sweden. Eight years after the Revolutionary War, both men found themselves involved in another revolution.

France had been in a state of unrest for some time, thanks to a shortage of food, an economic depression, and an ineffectual monarch—Louis XVI. In 1789, inspired by America's ex-

M̶W

Marie
Antoinette

Austrian,
1755-1793,
last queen of
France, executed
by guillotine
during the French
Revolution

ample, the French rose up against their king. The revolutionary national guard, commanded by the marquis de Lafayette, escorted Louis, his queen, and their children to the Tuileries Palace in Paris, where they remained virtual prisoners for the next four years.

The queen, Marie Antoinette, had learned ciphering skills from her mother, Maria Theresa of Austria, and from novels whose protagonists correspond through secret messages. The beautiful, spirited queen had a host of admirers, including Axel Fersen, the dashing Swedish hero of the American Revolution. Like the sweethearts in those romances, they exchanged enciphered love letters.

Though the nomenclator was still the reigning method of cryptography, Fersen devised a polyalphabetic cipher similar to Vigenère's tableau, but with the letters in pairs:

A	ab	cd	ef	gh	ik	lm	no	pq	rs	tu	xy	z&
B	bk	du	ei	fl	gn	ho	my	ps	qx	rt	ac	&z
C	lr	ad	bg	cz	s&	ek	fm	th	ix	np	oq	uy

WKH WZR UHYROXWLRQV

James
Monroe
....
American, 1758–1831,
soldier in the
Continental army and
Fifth President of
the United States

Like the Pretty Secure but Not Unbreakable method, Fersen's cipher switches alphabets with each plaintext letter, using a keyword as a guide. But to show you how it works, I'll use only the A alphabet. Suppose you want to encipher the word "Marie"; in place of the "m" you use the other letter in the pair, **l**. For the "a" you use its partner, **b**; for the "r", an **s**; for the "i", a **k**; for the "e", an **f**.

As the French Revolution grew more violent, the royal family feared for their lives. With Fersen's help, Marie Antoinette sent enciphered messages to relatives and friends, begging—unsuccessfully—for aid and support. In 1791, the royals escaped, disguised as servants, but were caught and imprisoned. The new government had intercepted and deciphered some of the queen's appeals. She and Louis were found guilty of plotting against the republic and beheaded on the notorious guillotine.

While France was still in the throes of its internal conflict, it began a series of campaigns (known as the French Revolutionary Wars) against other European powers. In 1803, the new French leader, Napoléon Bonaparte, desperate for funds, sold the vast territory of Louisiana to the newly formed United States.

James Monroe, then minister to France, helped conduct the

negotiations. He enciphered his correspondence using a nomenclator that became known as "Mr. Monroe's cypher" (the term *cypher* included both codes and ciphers). It was the nearest thing the United States had to an official diplomatic code.

Monroe's nomenclator consisted of some 1,700 words and syllables, each with a corresponding code number. Though it wasn't very secure—incredibly, it still listed words alphabetically and numbers in numerical order—American diplomats kept using it until after the Civil War.

Of course, no code is secure if the receiver can't be trusted. In 1806, former vice president Aaron Burr, bitter over the disgrace he'd brought on himself by killing Alexander Hamilton in a duel, conceived a rash plan; the exact details aren't clear, but apparently he meant to drive the Spanish out of the American Southwest and establish an independent empire there.

Among Burr's coconspirators was General James Wilkinson, temporary governor of the new Louisiana Territory. The two men corresponded using a clever and complex code made up of three different elements: a substitution cipher; a book code based on a popular dictionary; and symbols

Aaron Burr
American, 1756–1836,
Vice President to
Thomas Jefferson

that stood for commonly used words—for example, O meant "president," ☉ meant "vice president," and ÷ meant "secretary of state."

In October, Wilkinson received a coded dispatch from Burr, saying that he was on his way to Louisiana with sixty recruits. The governor—who was secretly being paid by the Spanish to protect their interests—betrayed his partner by sending a copy of the plaintext to President Jefferson. Burr and his men were captured, and Burr was tried for treason.

The dispatch was used as evidence against him. There were doubts, though, about how accurately Wilkinson had deciphered it, and Burr was acquitted. But in the court of public opinion, he was guilty. Threatened with death at the hands of a mob, Burr fled to Europe.

By the time of Burr and Jefferson, Europe and America were feeling the effects of the Industrial Revolution. New technologies—the steam engine, the power loom, the cotton gin—were transforming the lives of workers and farmers. In the 1830s, another mechanical device came along that transformed the art of cryptology by completely rewriting the rules.

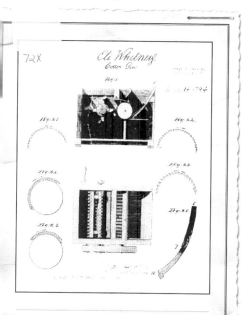

Patent Application for the Cotton Gin

CHAPTER EIGHT

Security Suffers Some Severe Setbacks

1837 CE – 1863 CE

For thousands of years, people had communicated mainly in writing—secret or otherwise—and relied on couriers or a postal service to deliver their messages. So if the courier wasn't waylaid or the mail wasn't opened and examined, the message was safe. The electric telegraph changed all that.

When the first electric battery appeared in 1800, scientists discovered that its current could deflect the needle of a compass. Using this principle, Englishmen William Cooke and Charles Wheatstone constructed the first practical telegraph system in 1837.

In 1844, American inventor and artist Samuel Morse developed a telegraph apparatus that contained an electromagnet. With it, he sent a series

Samuel Morse
....
American, 1791–1872, artist and inventor of the Morse Telegraph and Morse Code

RPH VHYHUH VHWEDFNV

of electrical pulses along a wire between Baltimore and Washington. The pulses—some short (dots), some long (dashes)—formed a binary code that became known as Morse code.

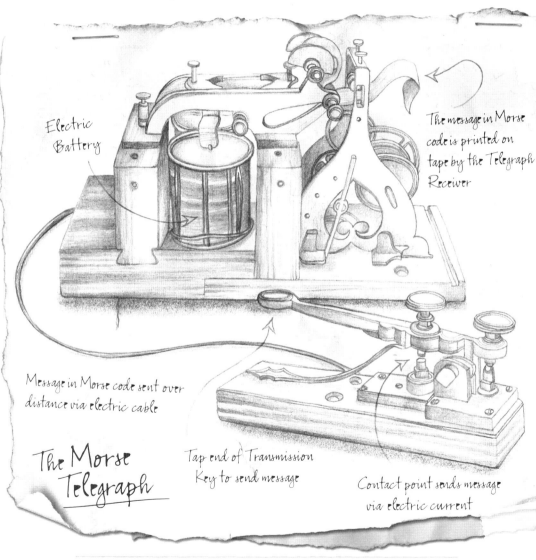

Electric Battery

The message in Morse code is printed on tape by the Telegraph Receiver

Message in Morse code sent over distance via electric cable

The Morse Telegraph

Tap end of Transmission Key to send message

Contact point sends message via electric current

By our definition, of course, it's not a code at all, but a monoalphabetic substitution cipher. And it certainly wasn't secret. Every telegraph operator could read it. As one English writer complained,

> Half-a-dozen people must be cognizant of every word addressed
> by one person to another. . . . Some simple yet secure cipher,
> easily acquired and easily read, should be introduced, by which
> means messages might to all intents and purposes be "sealed" to
> any person except the recipient.

The problem of how to keep a message private when you're sending it by very public means has continued to plague cryptographers and correspondents right up to the present day.

As people grew aware of the need for security, they took a new interest in cryptography and how it worked. In America, the fascination with codes and ciphers became something of a mania, thanks largely to the efforts of a popular writer of mystery and horror stories.

In 1839, Edgar Allan Poe issued a challenge to the readers of *Alexander's Weekly Messenger*, a Philadelphia newspaper. He declared that

> it is easy to decipher any species of hieroglyphical
> writing—that is to say writing where, in place of

INTERNATIONAL MORSE CODE

A	•—	S	•••
B	—•••	T	—
C	—•—•	U	••—
D	—••	V	•••—
E	•	W	•——
F	••—•	X	—••—
G	——•	Y	—•——
H	••••	Z	——••
I	••	1	•————
J	•———	2	••———
K	—•—	3	•••——
L	•—••	4	••••—
M	——	5	•••••
N	—•	6	—••••
O	———	7	——•••
P	•——•	8	———••
Q	——•—	9	————•
R	•—•	0	—————

VHFXULWB VXIIHUV VRPH VHYHUH VH

alphabetical letters, any kind of marks are made use of at random. . . . Let this be put to the test. Let any one address us a letter in this way, and we pledge ourselves to read it forthwith—however unusual or arbitrary may be the characters employed.

The response was overwhelming. Poe later wrote:

Letters were poured in upon the editor from all parts of the country; and many of the writers of these epistles were so convinced of the impenetrability of their mysteries, as to be at great pains to draw him into wagers on the subject. . . . There was only one which we did not immediately succeed in resolving. . . . We fully proved it a jargon of random characters, having no meaning whatever.

He concluded that "human ingenuity cannot concoct a cipher which human ingenuity cannot resolve." This may be true, but Poe himself wasn't all that ingenious. He had limited the challenge to monoalphabetic substitution ciphers, which can be cracked with relative ease using frequency analysis.

Nevertheless, many of his readers considered him "the most pro-found and skilful cryptographer who ever lived."

Poe enhanced his reputation with the classic short story "The Gold-Bug." The protagonist, William Legrand, lives on an island off the coast of South Carolina. One day he discovers a piece of parchment buried in the sand next to the remains of a boat. The parchment appears blank, but when it's held near a fire, the heat reveals a string of numbers and symbols written in invis-ible ink:

```
53‡‡†305))6*;4826)4‡.)4‡);806*;
48†8¶60))85;;]8*;:‡*8†83(88)5*†
;46(;88*96*?;8)*‡(;485);5*†2:*‡(
;4956*2(5*—4)8¶8*;4069285);)6†
8)4‡‡;1(‡9;48081;8:8‡1;48†85;4)
485†528806*81(‡9;48;(88;4(‡?34;
48)4‡;161;:188;‡?;
```

SPOILER WARNING: If you want to solve this cipher yourself, read no further, because the plain-text is revealed below! *Hint:* The most common letters in the message are "e" and "t."

Legrand is convinced that the parchment was left there by Cap-tain Kidd and contains directions to the pirate's buried treasure. (Apparently Poe didn't consider how unlikely it was that Captain

Kidd would use printers' symbols to encipher a message.) Using frequency analysis, Legrand discovers this message:

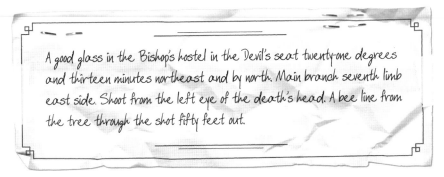

A good glass in the Bishop's hostel in the Devil's seat twenty-one degrees and thirteen minutes northeast and by north. Main branch seventh limb east side. Shoot from the left eye of the death's head. A bee line from the tree through the shot fifty feet out.

(*Glass* means telescope; the Devil's seat is a rock formation.) Legrand follows the instructions and digs up "an oblong chest of wood" containing "a treasure of incalculable value."

"The Gold-Bug" made cipher fanatics out of thousands of readers. When the story appeared in an anthology, two semi-colons in the middle of the second line were accidentally left out, so that "twenty" became "weny." Not a major problem, but it shows how easily errors can creep into a ciphertext. Suppose Captain Kidd had mistakenly put a **?** instead of a **(** in the word "north," making it "nouth." Poor Legrand wouldn't have known where to look.

Stage magician Robert Heller also did his part to popularize cryptography. He wasn't quite as obvious about it as Poe was. Very few theatregoers who caught Heller's "second sight" act realized that there were codes and ciphers involved.

The magician blindfolded his female assistant, then held up various objects contributed by members of the audience. The assistant described each object in detail, without seeing it. Here's how the trick worked.

Heller and the assistant memorized nineteen lists, each containing ten common items—a watch, a pipe, a glove, and so on. Heller indicated which list the item was on by saying a code phrase such as "**What is this?**" or "**Can you see this?**" He then used a code word that specified which item; if he said, for example, "**Be quick,**" the word **Be** meant number two on the list.

If the item wasn't on any list, Heller could spell its name, using a substitution cipher. Suppose he was handed a hat. For a plaintext "h," the cipher letter was an **I**. For the letter "a" he used an **H**; for a "t," a **P**. So Heller might say something like "**I**n my hand I have an object. **H**ave you any idea what it is? **P**lease tell me." **I H P** = h a t.

Meanwhile, in Russia, cryptography was being employed for a far more sinister purpose. Though Czar Alexander II had made many reforms, including the abolition of serfdom, a form of slavery, a group of revolutionaries called Nihilists were bent on destroying the monarchy. The conspirators corresponded using a system based on the Polybius checkerboard, with an added steganographic twist.

Suppose you're a Nihilist and you want to encipher the word

"czar." First you convert the letters into numbers, using the Polybius square from Chapter One: czar = **13 55 11 42**. Now, as in the Francis Bacon method, you need a longer passage to serve as your ciphertext—say, the Russian proverb "Those who walk softly go far." Write it out in normal handwriting, leaving small gaps between certain letters so the number of letters in each group matches the cipher numbers:

An upward stroke, as at the end of the word **go**, indicates the end of a group; a downward stroke, as at the end of **who**, means that the group includes some of the letters in the next word. So the **e** in **those**, the word **who**, and the **w** in **walk** are all part of the same five-letter group. (The **r** at the end of the sentence is a null.)

When Nihilists and other political dissidents were thrown into prison, they communicated with other prisoners though a "knock code," again based on the Polybius square. The letter "t," for example (**44** in Polybius's system), was conveyed by four quick knocks, a brief pause, then four more. In some prisons, the same system is still used today.

By the 1850s, the telegraph had spread its wires around the world and changed from a novelty to a necessity. Enterprising cryptographers did their best to provide a secure system that could be used over telegraph lines. Literally hundreds of nomenclators were published; some had only a few hundred entries, some as many as one hundred thousand. Unfortunately, they all had the same drawback: Anyone with a copy of the book could read the code.

The only really reliable system was the one developed by Vigenère nearly three centuries earlier, and the more paranoid used it to encipher their messages before giving them to the telegraph clerk. But Vigenère's tableau-and-keyword method had a fatal flaw, and in 1854 that flaw was discovered by a Cambridge mathematics professor.

Charles Babbage is best known as the inventor of the difference engine, the forerunner of the computer. But he had also been fascinated by cryptology ever since childhood:

Charles
Babbage

English,
1791–1871,
mathematician who
built the forerunner
to the computer: the
Difference engine

The bigger boys made ciphers, but if I got hold of a few words, I usually found out the key. The consequence

VHFXULWB VXIIHUV VRPH VHYHUH VHWEDFNV

of this ingenuity was occasionally painful: the owners of the detected ciphers sometimes thrashed me, though the fault lay in their own stupidity.

Babbage's discovery doesn't apply to the true *chiffre indéchiffrable*, which uses the plaintext itself as an autokey, only to the Pretty Secure version, which uses a repeating keyword. Babbage reasoned that if the keyword was short and the plaintext was long, a word that turned up over and over—"the," for example—was bound to get enciphered the same way more than once. These repeating chunks of ciphertext tell you how long the keyword is. Once you know that, you can deduce *what* the keyword is, and the jig is up. For a demonstration of Babbage's method, go to your nearest sidebar.

Unfortunately, Babbage never published his findings, so no one knew he'd broken the Vigenère cipher until very recently, when scholars began digging through his notes. Author Simon Singh suggests that Babbage may have been forced by the British government to keep his discovery

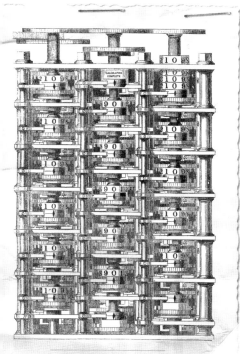

The Difference Engine

secret. England was battling Russia in the Crimean War at the time, and if the British alone knew how to break the "unbreakable" cipher, it would have given them a big advantage.

Whatever the reason, for a century and a half the credit for Vigenère's downfall went to Friedrich Kasiski, a retired Prussian army officer. Though Kasiski knew nothing of Babbage's work, he developed an identical technique, which he described in his 1863 book *Die Geheimschriften und die Dechiffrierkunst* (*Secret Writing and the Art of Deciphering*).

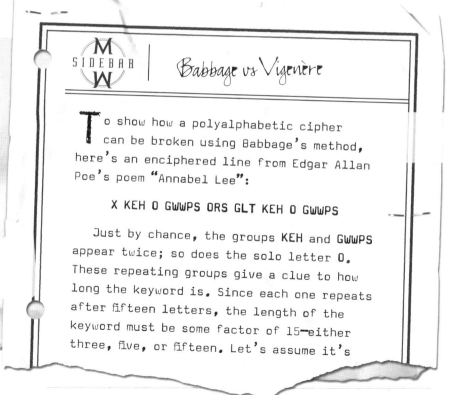

Babbage vs Vigenère

To show how a polyalphabetic cipher can be broken using Babbage's method, here's an enciphered line from Edgar Allan Poe's poem "Annabel Lee":

X KEH O GWWPS ORS GLT KEH O GWWPS

Just by chance, the groups KEH and GWWPS appear twice; so does the solo letter O. These repeating groups give a clue to how long the keyword is. Since each one repeats after fifteen letters, the length of the keyword must be some factor of 15—either three, five, or fifteen. Let's assume it's

VHFXULWB VXIIHUV VRPH VHYHUH VHWEDFNV

three letters long. That means every third letter is enciphered using the same alphabet.

That lonesome letter O is most likely an "a," the most common one-letter word. In Vigenère's tableau (page 43), a plaintext "a" is replaced by a ciphertext O in the O alphabet. So every third letter must also be enciphered using the O alphabet. Look them up on the tableau and you get these plaintext letters:

X wEH a GWiPS aRS sLT wEH a GWiPS

aRS is pretty sure to be "and," the second most common three-letter word. In the tableau, "n" is enciphered as R using the E alphabet, and "d" is enciphered as S using the P alphabet. So we now know that the three letters of the keyword are O, E, and P—POE, actually. Convert the X, H, W, S, T, H, W, and S using the P alphabet and the E, G, P, L, E, G, and P using the E alphabet and you've got the entire plaintext.[*] Simple, right? Sure, when somebody shows you how it's done. But imagine figuring it out from scratch, the way Babbage did. No wonder he's considered a genius.

[*] I was a child and she was a child.

CHAPTER NINE

The Blue and the Gray (and the Green and the Brown)

1863 CE – 1883 CE

Telegraph wires in
New York c. 1890

I n changing forever the art of communication, the telegraph also transformed the business of war. For the first time in history, commanders could send unlimited messages rapidly over long distances; this meant they could better control the movements of vast numbers of soldiers and efficiently supply them with weapons and food.

Of course, the telegraph had one serious shortcoming: The enemy could cut the wires or, even worse, tap into them and intercept messages. A secure code or cipher was more vital than ever.

Friedrich Kasiski had just demolished the most effective cipher known. As far as American military leaders were concerned, he couldn't have published his groundbreaking work at a worse time. They were in the most crucial stage of the Civil War; if they couldn't conceal their plans and troop movements from the enemy, the results could be disastrous.

WKH EOXH DQG WKH JUDB DQG
WKH JUHHQ DQG WKH EURZQ

Confederate soldier   Union soldier

But the fact is, security is defined differently on the battlefield than it is in civilian life. As mathematician W. W. Rouse Ball points out, in war "a system is generally considered sufficiently secure if the delay caused the enemy in its attempts at solution is long enough to make the information valueless." In other words, once the orders have been carried out, it doesn't matter whether the enemy can read them or not. So most armies make do with a *field cipher* that's not intended to be unbreakable, just tough enough to buy the sender some time.

The Union army was not only better fed and equipped than the Confederates; it had better codes and ciphers. The North's favorite field cipher was actually a combination nomenclator and transposition cipher conceived by Anson Stager, former head of Western Union Telegraph Company. Instead of transposing letters, as the ancient scytale did, Stager transposed entire words. As he knew from his telegraphic experience, words are less likely to get garbled in transmission.

Here's an example, based on an actual message sent by Abraham Lincoln: "Correspondents of the Tribune **WAYLAND** at **NEPTUNE**. Please ascertain why they are detained and get them off if you can." **WAYLAND** is a codeword for "captured;" **NEPTUNE** is Richmond, the Confederate capital. The words are arranged in columns, with nulls at the bottom of each column:

correspondents	of	the	Tribune
WAYLAND	at	**NEPTUNE**	please
ascertain	why	they	are
detained	and	get	them
off	if	you	can
THIS	**FILLS**	**IT**	**UP**

To create a ciphertext, the words are transcribed in a different order, using a predetermined route (the system is often called a *route cipher*). Begin with the word **THIS** and go up, then down, then up, then down, and you get this:

THIS OFF DETAINED ASCERTAIN WAYLAND CORRESPONDENTS OF AT WHY AND IF FILLS IT YOU GET THEY NEPTUNE THE TRIBUNE PLEASE ARE THEM CAN UP

The code may not seem very secure, but apparently it did the trick. Using this and other methods, Union commanders sent more than *six million* coded dispatches; if the enemy deciphered a single one, there's no record of it. Frustrated by their lack of

WKH EOXH DQG WKH JUDB DQG
WKH JUHHQ DQG WKH EURZQ

success, Confederate cryptanalysts printed intercepted Yankee messages in Southern newspapers, hoping in vain that some clever reader might manage to break them.

The South had no official code or cipher. Officers decided for themselves what method to use, and most of their cryptograms were easy pickings for Union cryptanalysts. The messages sometimes baffled other Southerners, though. After trying for twelve hours to unravel a Vigenère cipher, one Rebel officer gave up and rode his horse around enemy lines to talk to the sender in person.

Confederate cryptographers weren't quite as hopeless as they may sound. They used some clever steganographic ploys, including one that, a century later, became an essential tool of Cold War espionage: microphotography. During the Civil War, the United States consul in Toronto reported that some Rebel couriers to Canada wore "metal buttons, which, upon the inside, dispatches are most minutely photographed, not perceptable [sic] to the naked eye, but are easily read by the aid of a powerful lens."

Buttons from Confederate soldiers' uniforms were used to hide microdots.

The Rebs also rediscovered Alberti's disk. But thanks to Kasiski, cryptanalysts could now crack a polyaphabetic cipher, so the Alberti disk was no more secure than the Vigenère tableau.

Both sides made frequent use of spies, and some of the most resourceful were women. "Rebel Rose" Greenhow, widow of a prominent Washington doctor, eavesdropped on Union officers, then conveyed the information to the Confederacy by female couriers. They carried the dispatches in secret pockets or concealed in their hair, which was braided and wrapped in a tight bun. Greenhow's reports helped ensure a Southern victory at the first battle of Bull Run.

Even after she and her young daughter were imprisoned by Union forces, Rebel Rose went on sending secret messages; she hid them inside her daughter's rubber ball, which she then tossed through a window of the prison to a waiting Rebel agent.

Spies on both sides used invisible ink, substitution ciphers, and route ciphers. One favorite transposition method was called the *rail fence cipher* because its zigzag pattern looked like a split log fence as seen from above. To encipher Mark Twain's famous quote "Man is the only animal that blushes. Or needs to," first stagger the letters like this:

WKH EOXH DQG WKH JUDB DQG
WKH JUHHQ DQG WKH EURZQ

```
M n s h o l a i a t a b u h s r e d t
  a i t e n y n m l h t l s e o n e s o
```

**Abraham
Lincoln**
....
American,
1809-1865,
16th President
of the United
States

Convert it to ciphertext by writing the first line in groups of five letters, then the second line: **Mnsho laiat abuhs redta iteny nmlht lseon eso**. The receiver just divides the message into equal halves and prints the first letter of the left half, then the first letter of the right half, then the second letter of the left half, and so on.

If you'd like to tear down a rail fence, here's an enciphered quote from American author Henry David Thoreau: **Itksw tsekh tuhnt sekna ohroe rtaet oopat ertoe opaad nteth a** * (when the cryptogram has an odd number of letters, divide it so there's one more letter in the left part than in the right).

Near the end of the war, a group of Southern sympathizers conspired to assassinate President Lincoln. There's evidence that they may have used a cipher to help keep their plan a secret. After the assassin, actor John Wilkes Booth, was killed, investigators searched his room at the National Hotel in Washington and discovered in his traveling trunk a Vigenère tableau.

MYSTERIOUS MESSAGES   98

* It takes two to speak the truth—one to speak and another to hear.

Some historians think that Lincoln's assassination was part of a plot mas-terminded by his secretary of war, Edwin Stanton, who felt the president was being too soft on the South.

In 1962, a Civil War buff named Ray Neff uncovered evidence that supports this theory. In an 1864 issue of *Colburn's United Service Magazine*, Neff found two curious cryptograms. One was a monoalpha-betic cipher scrawled in the margins of the magazine. There were also tiny dots un-der certain letters of the printed text—a variation of Aeneas the Tactician's an-cient pinhole method. The plaintext read, in part:

> It was on the tenth of April, Sisty-five [sic] when I first knew that the plan was in action. . . . the deed to be done of the forteenth [sic]. I did not know the identity of the assas-sin but I knew most all else when I approached E. S. about it. . . . There were at least eleven members of Con-

WKH EOXH DQG WKH JUDB DQG
WKH JUHHQ DQG WKH EURZQ

gress involved in the plot. . . . I fear for my life. L.C.B.

Lincoln's assassination took place on April 14, 1865. The entries were dated February 5, 1868. A test for invisible ink revealed the signature of Lafayette C. Baker, former head of the Union's counterintelligence unit. Baker died in 1868 under suspicious circumstances; a list of his possessions included issues of *Colburn's* Magazine for the years 1860 to 1865.

The year after the Civil War ended, American businessman Cyrus Field laid the first successful transatlantic telegraph cable. Suddenly correspondents in Europe and North America could exchange messages at the speed of an electric current. And

William Seward pictured with his daughter, Fanny.

just as suddenly the ubiquitous Monroe Cypher, designed for written communications, became obsolete.

Secretary of State William Seward found out just how impractical the old code was when he cabled a dispatch to the United States minister in France. To avoid confusion, the code numbers had to be spelled out. A State Department memo noted that "from fifteen to twenty letters . . . are necessary to express a single letter of the cypher."

It took telegraph operators several hours to transmit Seward's 3,722-word cryptogram, and they made no fewer than thirty-five errors. The cost of sending the message: $1,833. The lesson cryptographers learned from the experience: priceless.

The shamefaced Seward commissioned a more efficient State Department code that replaced common words with a single letter or two. This method had its own problems and was replaced by the Red Cipher (so called because of its red cover), which substituted code words for plaintext words. A rainbow of other ciphers followed—the Blue, the Green, the Gray, the Brown. Some had to be scrapped because a foreign agent had stolen a copy of the codebook.

Stealing a country's codes may seem underhanded, but it's nothing compared to the dirty tricks American politicians pulled during the presidential race of 1876. Republican candidate Rutherford B. Hayes was pitted against the Democratic governor of New York, Samuel J. Tilden, in what author and code expert Fred Wrixon calls "the most bitterly disputed presidential election in American history."

There were doubts about the accuracy of vote counts in some states, so Congress created a special election commission to decide the outcome. When the commission declared Hayes the

WKH EOXH DQG WKH JUDB DQG
WKH JUHHQ DQG WKH EURZQ

Rutherford B. Hayes   Samuel J. Tilden

winner, Tilden's supporters accused the Republicans of fraud. The truth, as it turned out, was quite the contrary.

Investigators uncovered a number of enciphered telegrams sent to and from prominent Democrats. Some were transposition ciphers, some were monoalphabetic substitutions, others used a dictionary-based book code. When deciphered, the telegrams proved that Tilden's men had bribed election officials in at least four states. Tilden denied any knowlege of the bribes, but his career was ruined.

Though people were using cryptography in record numbers, it's clear from the Tilden incident that most weren't very good at it. Amateur cryptographers have a bad habit of overestimating the security of their ciphers. As David Kahn writes, "Few false ideas have more firmly gripped the minds of so many intelligent men than the one that, if they just tried, they could invent a cipher that no one could break."

In 1883, a Dutch linguist named Auguste Kerckhoffs published a book titled *La Cryptographie Militaire*, which explored in depth the principles of cryptography and addressed the challenges presented by the telegraph.

Kerckhoffs listed six basic requirements of a reliable cipher system: 1) It should be, for all practical purposes, unbreakable. 2) If the system is compromised, it shouldn't cause trouble for the correspondents. 3) The key should be easily remembered and easily changed. 4) The ciphertext should be easy to transmit telegraphically. 5) If a cipher device is involved, one person should be able work it and transport it easily. 6) The system should be simple to use.

Kerckhoffs was the first to point out that even if the enemy knows what basic method, or *algorithm*, you're using, it doesn't necessarily mean the cipher is useless. "The security of a cryptosystem," he wrote, "must not depend on keeping secret the algorithm used in the system, but only on keeping the key secret."

Suppose, for example, you're using an Alberti disk; the enemy might have an identical disk, but it's no big thing as long he doesn't know what key letter you're using. Even in the computer age, Kerckhoffs's principle remains the fundamental rule of cryptography.

Auguste
Kerckhoffs

Dutch, 1835-1903,
author and
cryptographer

WKH EOXH DQG WKH JUDB DQG
WKH JUHHQ DQG WKH EURZQ

CHAPTER TEN

Agony, Dancing Men, and Buried Treasure

Since Kerckhoffs's work was written mainly for the military, the general public wasn't aware of it. Most people went on putting their faith in flimsy ciphers. Some of the flimsiest appeared in the personal columns of English newspapers—known as the "agony columns" because so many entries were from heartsick lovers kept apart by the strict moral standards of Victorian society.

The messages often substituted numbers for plaintext in a painfully obvious fashion—for example, **1** for "a," **2** for "b," and so on. Several noted cryptographers—including Charles Babbage and telegraph pioneer Sir Charles Wheatstone—amused themselves by deciphering the entries.

Wheatstone took a special interest in the cryptograms an Oxford student named Charlie sent to his London sweetheart. When Charlie asked the girl to elope, Wheatstone placed a personal ad of his own, using the same cipher, advising her not to go through with it. Soon afterward a note from the girl appeared in the column: "Dear Charlie, Write no more. Our cipher is discovered."

The papers also carried ciphers devised by amateur cryptologists who, like Poe, challenged readers to solve them. Penny-wise Victorians sometimes used newspapers as a cheap way of corresponding with friends; as Aeneas the Tactitian advised, they poked tiny holes beneath individual letters to spell out their message, then sent the entire newspaper, which could be mailed for free.

Book cover from an 1860s edition of Jules Verne's *Five Weeks in a Balloon*, and *Journey to the Center of the Earth*.

Cryptography was turning up regularly as a plot device in popular literature. The hero of Jules Verne's 1885 novel *Mathias Sandorf* employs a Cardano-type grille, which the author probably learned about from reading Kerckhoffs. In A *Journey to the Center of the Earth*, Verne has the narrator's uncle discover a "mysterious parchment" covered with symbols that, when he converts them to English letters, reveal this meaningless message:

DJRQB, GDQFLQJ PHQ, DQG EXULHG WUHDVXUH

The uncle is ready to call it quits, but then the narrator happens to look at the paper from behind and realizes that, if read in reverse, the letters form Latin words. When translated, the message says

Descend into the crater of Yocul of Sneffels, which the shade of Scartaris caresses, before the kalends of July, audacious traveler, and you will reach the center of the earth. I did it.

ARNE SAKNUSSEMM

Sir Arthur Conan Doyle's famous fictional detective Sherlock Holmes claims that he is "fairly familiar with all forms of secret writings, and am myself the author of a trifling monograph upon the subject, in which I analyse one hundred and sixty separate ciphers." Doyle gives him three opportunities to display his skills.

In the novel *The Valley of Fear*, the detective has to solve a cryptogram made up of numbers. "There are many ciphers which I would read as easily as I do the apocrypha of the agony column," says Holm-

Sherlock Holmes

es. "But this is different. It is clearly a reference to the words in a page of some book. Until I am told which page and which book I am powerless." He finally deduces that the book used as the key is *Whitaker's Almanac.*

Sir Arthur Conan Doyle
English, 1859–1930, author of the Sherlock Holmes detective series

The short story "The *Gloria Scott*" presents the detective with a null cipher, "one of those ingenious secret codes which mean one thing while they seem to mean another." The awkwardly worded cryptogram reads:

> *The supply of game for London is going steadily up. Head-keeper Hudson, we believe, has been now told to receive all orders for fly-paper and for preservation of your hen-pheasants' life.*

Holmes tries reading the text backward, then reading every other word. It's only when you read every third word (starting with *The* and ignoring the hyphens) that the true message is revealed.

In "The Adventure of the Dancing Men," stick figures that appear to be a child's scrawl are in fact a monoalphabetic substitute cipher. Though the messages are too brief for frequency analysis, Holmes deciphers them with the help of some shrewd guesses, then creates a fake message to trick the villain. But Holmes's dancing men can't manage to get the steps quite right. His cryptogram, shown below, was supposed to read, "Come here at once."

What it actually says is "Mome here at onme."

An 1885 publication titled "The Beale Papers" contains cryptograms that are in a whole different league from those devised by Conan Doyle and Verne. They continue to this day to defy solution.

The author of the twenty-three-page pamphlet declines to identify himself "to avoid the multitude of letters with which I should be assailed . . . requiring answers which, if attended to, would absorb my entire time." Though he claims that the tale the booklet tells is true, it rivals any fiction ever written by Poe.

In 1822, the story goes, Robert Morriss, an innkeeper in Lynchburg, Virginia, rented a room for several months to an adventurer named Thomas Jefferson Beale. Before the lodger left, he gave Morriss a locked iron box for safekeeping. If Beale didn't return within ten years, the innkeeper was to open the box and read the enciphered contents, with the help of a cipher key that Beale promised to send later.

Morriss never saw the man again, or the promised cipher key. In 1845, he finally broke the box open, to find three pages of numbers plus a plaintext note from Beale.

Three years before he met Morriss, Beale said, he took a hunting party to what is now New Mexico. They discovered huge deposits of gold and silver, which they dug up, carted back to Virginia, and buried. One of the pages of numbers was a cipher revealing the exact location of the treasure. The second described the contents of the treasure chests. The third was a list of Beale's partners, each of whom was entitled to a share. But without the key, Morriss could make no sense of the numbers.

In 1862, he passed the papers on to a friend—the anonymous author of "The Beale Papers"—who guessed the numbers were part of a book code. "With this idea," he wrote, "a test was made of every book I could procure . . . all to no purpose, however, until the Declaration of Independence afforded the clue to one of the papers, and revived all my hopes."

Beale had numbered all of the Declaration's 1,322 words; each number in the ciphertext stood for the first letter of the

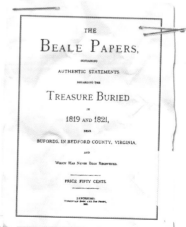

Cover of The Beale Papers

DJRQB, GDQFLQJ PHQ, DQG EXU

corresponding word. Since *necessary* is the tenth word in the Declaration, the cipher number **10** stands for *n*.

With this key, Anonymous Author cracked cipher number two, which described the treasure. But apparently Beale had used a different key for number three and for number one—the crucial cipher, since it gave directions to the treasure. A.A. devoted so much time to the puzzle that he was "reduced from comparative affluence to absolute penury." Finally he "resolved to sever at once, and forever, all connection with the affair" and "determined to make public the whole matter."

He warned the reader "to devote only such time as can be spared from your legitimate business to the task, and if you can spare no time, let the matter alone." Despite the warning—and the possibility that the whole thing was a hoax—countless cryptographers and treasure seekers have spent much of their lives and fortunes trying to break the cipher and locate the hidden hoard, whose value is estimated at over $40 million.

As the nineteenth century drew to a close, Italian inventor Guglielmo Marconi began work on a device that would have even more colossal consequences for communications, cryptic and otherwise, than the telegraph had.

An early Marconi Radio receiver

CHAPTER ELEVEN

The Manuscript, the Machine, and the Mexican Message

1901 CE – 1924 CE

I n the 1880s, German physicist Heinrich Hertz began experimenting with high-frequency electromagnetic waves, or radio waves. But Guglielmo Marconi was the first to use radio waves to send wireless messages over long distances. In 1901, he transmitted the Morse-code signal for the letter "s" from a base in Cornwall, England. It was picked up in St. John's, Newfoundland, all the way across the Atlantic.

As if messages sent over a wire weren't vulnerable enough, now they were being broadcast through the air. Military commanders recognized at once both the possibilities and the problems of radio. The upside was that armies could communicate more easily; the downside was,

Guglielmo Marconi
Italian, 1874–1937, inventor and radio pioneer

the enemy could intercept or disrupt those communications more easily.

The new medium got its trial by fire during World War I. In 1914, at the very outset of the war, the British cut Germany's transatlantic telegraph cables. For the next four years German officers and diplomats had two choices: They could send messages over telegraph cables controlled by their enemies, or they could send them using radio waves.

The Germans had a fairly secure code—a nomenclator with code words that were themselves enciphered by monoalphabetic substitution. But in September 1914, the Russian navy recovered the body of a German officer from a sunken ship. Clasped in the corpse's arms were copies of the German code. The Russians turned the material over to British intelligence's codebreaking branch, known as Room 40.

A British admiral called Room 40's cryptanalysts "perhaps the most brilliant lot of young people ever brought together." At the beginning of the war, few had any real experience cracking ciphers, but they learned quickly. Within weeks, they were regularly reading the German navy's dispatches. They also broke several German diplomatic codes. In January 1917, they intercepted one of the most crucial cryptograms of all time—the Zimmermann telegram.

Two years earlier, a German submarine had torpedoed the

Lusitania, a British passenger ship. Twelve hundred people drowned, including 128 Americans. United States president Woodrow Wilson, determined to

The Lusitania

keep his country out of the war, took no action beyond a strong protest. The German foreign minister, Arthur Zimmermann, promised there would be no more attacks on civilian vessels.

But in 1917, Germany resumed unrestricted submarine warfare. Knowing this might goad Wilson into declaring war, Zimmermann hatched a nasty plan to distract the United States: He would persuade Mexico to invade its northern neighbor in hopes of reclaiming the territory that Mexico lost during the Mexican-American War.

Zimmermann outlined his plan in an enciphered telegram to the German ambassador in Washington, D.C., who forwarded it to the ambassador in Mexico. Since Germany's overseas cables were kaput, Zimmermann had to use cables controlled by Sweden and America. Both were monitored by Room 40.

When British codebreakers deciphered the message, they realized the impact it could have

Arthur Zimmermann

WKH PDQXVFULSW WK. DQG WKH PHA DQ HVVDJH

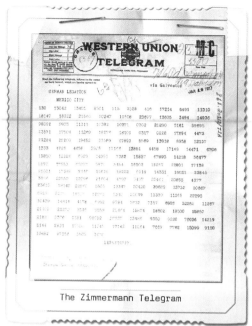

The Zimmermann Telegram

on the war. But if they made the telegram public, Germany would know its code was no longer secure. British intelligence devised a devious plan of its own. It instructed a British agent to infiltrate the Mexican telegraph office and steal the telegram that had been forwarded from Washington. It had been re-enciphered using an older, simpler German code.

A copy of this version was sent to President Wilson, who demanded to know whether the message was genuine. "I cannot deny it," replied Zimmerman. "It is true." In April 1917, the United States entered the war and helped turn the tide against Germany.

When it came to cryptological expertise, though, the Americans didn't contribute much to World War I. The War Department had a Military Intelligence Division, known as MI-8, but no official bureau for making and breaking codes. American troops used a variety of cryptographic methods, none of them very secure.

One unauthorized code used baseball terminology. If the Germans—many of whom idolized German composer Richard Wagner—shelled an American position, the radioman reported

WAGNER AT BAT; if the bombardment was heavy, the message was **WAGNER KNOCKED A HOME RUN**. Overall, American soldiers had little patience with codes and ciphers. When they did use them, they were so careless that one officer remarked, "There certainly never existed . . . a force more negligent in the use of their own code than was the American Army."

The same year that saw the end of World War I saw the development of what code expert Simon Singh calls "the Holy Grail of cryptography"—a truly unbreakable cipher known as the *one-time pad*.

As Babbage and Kasiski pointed out, the flaw in any polyalphabetic cipher is the repeating keyword. Even a keyword that's as long as the plaintext presents problems. The example of the second Beale Cipher shows that if you figure out what text the sender used as a key, you're home free.

But what if the key is some totally random sequence of letters? That's the essence of the one-time pad cipher. The sender and the receiver have identical pads of paper with blocks of random letters or numbers on each page. Let's say page one looks like this:

G	B	W	L	P	V	N
D	H	I	P	K	D	X
R	J	S	W	M	G	A
Y	Z	M	D	Y	E	V
K	G	S	O	D	Q	H

WKH PDQXVFULSW, WKH PDFKLQH
DQG WKH PHALFDQ PHVVDJH

Now, suppose you're Arthur Zimmermann and you want to encipher this proposal to Mexico: "Make war together, make peace together." Write the letters of the key above the letters of the plaintext, then consult the Vigenère tableau on page 43.

Key:	G B W L P V N D H I P K D X R J S W M G A Y Z M D Y E V K G S O
Plaintext:	M A K E W A R T O G E T H E R M A K E P E A C E T O G E T H E R
Cipher:	S B G P L V E W V O T D K B I V S G Q V E Y B Q W M K Z D N W F

Even though the words "make" and "together" repeat, there's no repetition in the ciphertext. (E, K and T are enciphered the same way more than once, but that doesn't give a cryptanalyst much to work with.) Each time you send a message, you use a new sheet of the pad and each sheet has a new block of random letters.

Like most ciphers and codes, the one-time pad has its drawbacks. It's time-consuming to print page after page of random letters, and hard to get them completely random. And, as with a nomenclator, if the enemy gets hold of the pad, you're in big trouble. Still, if Zimmermann had been able to use the system, World War I might have turned out quite differently.

Herbert Yardley, head of America's MI-8, recognized the value of the one-time pad, but couldn't convince the State Department to adopt it. He did get the government to establish a "permanent organization for code and cipher investigation and attack" and put him in charge. Yardley wrote that the American Black Chamber "sees all, hears all. . . . Its sensitive ears catch the faintest whisperings in the foreign capitals of the world."

Over the next twelve years, the American Chamber's cryptologists deciphered more than forty-five thousand secret messages from nearly every major country. But it wasn't enough to satisfy them. In their spare time Yardley and his assistant, John Manly, tried to break the two unsolved Beale Ciphers as well as another famous ciphertext—the Voynich manuscript, which Manly called "the most mysterious manuscript in the world."

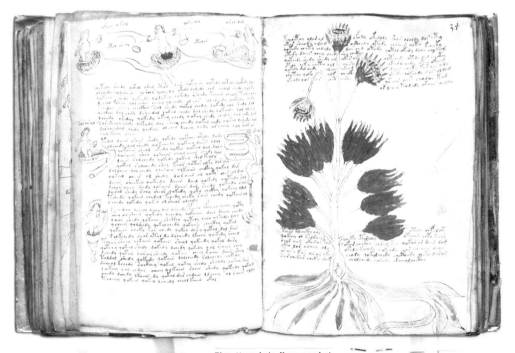

The Voynich Manuscript

The Voynich appears to date from the late Middle Ages or the Renaissance. Its two hundred pages are covered with odd diagrams and drawings—in the words of author and historian Ronald Lewin, "a bizarre mixture of astronomical figures, plants and bulbous human figures"—plus a handwritten text that resembles no known language.

The manuscript's origins are as enigmatic as its contents. Its first known owner was Holy Roman Emperor Rudolph II, who purchased it in the late sixteenth or early seventeenth century, possibly from Queen Elizabeth's physician, Dr. John Dee. According to a writer of the time, Dee had a "book containing nothing but hieroglyphicks" that he "bestowed much time upon, but I could not hear that he could make it out."

After Rudolph's death, the book fell into the hands of Johannes Marci, rector of the University of Prague. Marci believed its author was the thirteenth-century friar Roger Bacon—who, you recall, advocated writing down dangerous knowledge in secret script.

Unable to decipher the manuscript, in 1666 Marci passed it on to scholar Athanasius Kircher, who had no better luck. Kircher donat-

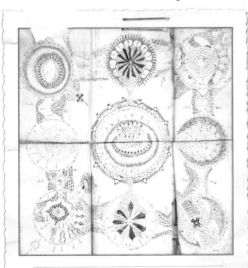

A six-page fold out from the Voynich Manuscript, showing what is thought to be astronomical diagrams.

ed it to a Jesuit college, where it lay until 1912, when American rare-book dealer Wilfrid Voynich discovered and bought it.

Voynich sent photocopies of the manuscript to scholars, scientists, and linguists, hoping they could shed some light on it. William Newbold, a professor of philosophy, examined the text under a magnifying glass and found what seemed to be tiny shorthand symbols. Using a convoluted process, he translated the symbols into Latin sentences that supposedly proved the book was the work of Roger Bacon.

But when John Manly of the Black Chamber studied the manuscript, he pronounced Newbold's "shorthand symbols" nothing more than cracks in the paper and fragments of ink. Manly concluded that Newbold was "a victim of his own intense enthusiasm and his learned and ingenious subconscious." Like the Beale Cipher, the Voynich manuscript has gone on tantalizing and thwarting cryptographers to this day.

• • •   • — — •   • —   — • — •   •

In 1922, the U.S. Army finally adopted a reliable cipher device that soldiers could use in the field. The device—which the army, in typical unimaginative military fashion, dubbed the M-94— consisted of twenty-five silver-dollar-size aluminum disks lined up on a spindle. Each disk had a mixed alphabet printed around the circumference. Sound familiar? Yes, it was a dead ringer for

Thomas Jefferson's wheel cypher, even though Jefferson's design hadn't been discovered yet.

At the same time this simple device was being developed, several inventors, using the same basic principles, were building machines that were far more complex and high-tech. The most successful was called the Enigma.

An early version, the *Geheimschrijfmachine* (secret writing machine), had been patented in 1919 by Dutch inventor Hugo Koch. Koch sold the patent rights to German electrical engineer and cryptologist Arthur Scherbius, who improved the design and marketed it to business people. His advertising flyer boasted, "The natural inquisitiveness of competitors is at once checkmated by a machine that enables you to keep all your documents . . . entirely secret."

Though the Enigma was secure, its hefty price tag put off potential buyers. Scherbius offered it to the military, but the Germans considered their current system good enough. When they finally learned that the British had cracked their code, they bought Scherbius's machines as fast as he could produce them.

The Enigma resembles a typewriter sitting atop a miniature version of the old plug boards once used by telephone operators. In simple terms, it's an electronic version of the Alberti disk or the Vigenère tableau. When you type a plaintext letter, a ciphertext letter lights up on a display at the rear of keyboard. The electrical circuits inside change with each letter you type, producing a polyalphabetic cipher without the effort of using a disk or tableau, and without the problems inherent in using a keyword. If you want to know more, see the sidebar.

SIDEBAR M W

The Rotor Router

At the heart of the Enigma and similar machines are several gizmos called rotors. They're similar to the alphabet disks in the M-94 and Jefferson's wheel cypher, except they're made of hard rubber and next to each letter is a pair of electrical contacts, one on each side of the rotor.

The early Engimas have three rotors. Hit the A on the keyboard and it sends an electric current to the A on rotor number one. But wiring inside the rotor makes the current emerge at a different point—let's say the X. The current winds around through rotor number two and emerges at yet another point—the M, perhaps—then through rotor number three, which might spit it out at the contact marked P. From there, the current goes to a lamp board, where it lights up P, your first ciphertext letter.

So far, the machine seems like nothing more than a gee-whiz way of creating a monoalphabetic cipher. But it's not.

Because each time you hit a key, rotor number one turns one notch. It's doing automatically the same thing you do when you use the Vigenère tableau with a keyword—switching to a new cipher alphabet with each letter. Except the Engima never repeats itself, because each time rotor number one goes around 360 degrees, it turns rotor number two one notch. And when rotor number two makes a full turn, it moves rotor number three one notch.

The Enigma has several other tricks that make it even more secure: 1) You can switch the position of the rotors. 2) Each rotor has twenty-six possible starting positions; you can start with the A facing upward, or the M, or whatever. With these two features, you can arrange the rotors in any one of 17,576 ways. 3) Between the keyboard and rotor number one is a plug board with six cables that determine which contact on the rotor the current will flow to; change the position of a cable, and the whole route changes.

Obviously, even if you have an identical machine, you have to know exactly what settings the sender used in order for it to work right.

Interchangeable Rotors

Lampboard
(displays ciphertext letter)

Keyboard

The Enigma Machine

Plugboard

WKH PDQXVFULSW, WKH PDFKLQH
DQG WKH PHALFDQ PHVVDJH

CHAPTER TWELVE

Romance, Rum, and *Romaji*

—— 1924 CE – 1939 CE ——

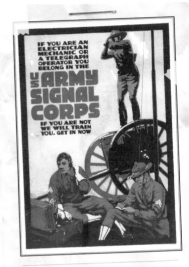

A 1920s recruitment poster for the US Army Signal Corps

In 1924, the American military, which was already monitoring radio transmissions from a dozen foreign countries, turned its attention to new territory—outer space. Mars was making its nearest approach to Earth, and at the request of a noted astronomer, Signal Corps operators searched the radio waves, listening for patterns that might indicate the Martians were trying to communicate with us.

They heard nothing more startling than some human radio tests. But according to a *New York Times* article, a civilian who aimed a radio camera at the red planet recorded "a fairly regular arrangement of dots and dashes" and some "curiously jumbled groups, each taking the form of a crudely drawn face."

The civilian asked William Friedman, the Signal Corps' chief codebreaker, to see if he could make any sense of the signals. "I thought him a sort of visionary," said Friedman, "and didn't try to do anything with his record. I was probably wrong!"

It was one of the few cryptological challenges Friedman passed up in his long and varied career. In the decades that followed, he became a leading authority on codes and ciphers and helped turn cryptanalysis from a form of guesswork into a science, ruled by the principles of mathematics and statistics.

• • •   • — — •   • —   — • — •   •

William Friedman didn't set out to be a cryptologist. He studied genetics at Cornell University. In 1915, he began working for wealthy businessman George Fabyan, improving the crops and livestock on Fabyan's Illinois farm. Soon Friedman got involved in another of his boss's pet projects—proving that Shakespeare's plays were written by Francis Bacon.

Supervising the project was a young woman named Elizabeth Smith. At first she bought Fabyan's theory that the plays were one huge cryptogram devised by Bacon. But later she admitted, "Neither I nor any other one of the industrious research workers . . . ever succeeded in extracting a single

William Friedman
American, 1891–1969, called the Dean of American Cryptography

Elizebeth
Friedman

American,
1892-1980,
pioneering
cryptanalyst

long sentence of a hidden message." One good thing came out of the experience, though: She and coworker William Friedman fell in love. They married in 1917.

When the Friedmans quit the Shakespeare project, William took a job with the Signal Corps. By 1922, he was in charge of the code and cipher department. Two years later, he played a small but crucial role in a famous American political scandal.

The Teapot Dome scandal took its name from a government oil field in Wyoming. Though the oil was earmarked for use by the U.S. Navy, Secretary of the Interior Albert Fall leased the field to a private company, Pan American Petroleum. In return, Pan American gave Secretary Fall $100,000, using Edward McLean, editor of the *Washington Post*, as a middleman.

A Senate investigation turned up coded telegrams sent to and from McLean. William Friedman was asked to decode them. He discovered that McClean's code was a nomenclator used by the Department of Justice's Bureau of Investigation (forerunner of the FBI). Both Edward McClean and his private secretary had once been special agents of the Justice Department. McClean insisted that the $100,000 he gave Secretary Fall was just a loan, but the telegrams proved it was a bribe from Pan American, and Fall went to jail.

Though the Teapot Dome cryptograms weren't much of a stretch for Friedman, he found others that truly challenged his skills. One was the Beale Cipher. He was just as stumped by it as his colleagues at the Black Chamber had been.

Friedman also tackled ciphers created by American inventor Edward Hebern's Enigma-style machine. Using complicated techniques, Friedman figured out how the machine's five rotors were wired. The lessons he learned from deconstructing Hebern's machine would prove invaluable during World War II, when Friedman was struggling to break Japanese military codes.

But in the 1920s, America was at war only with gangsters, bootleggers, and rumrunners. Due to a new constitutional amendment that prohibited the manufacture, sale, or transportation of alcoholic beverages, there was a flourishing black market for liquor.

Rumrunners smuggled in much of the illegal booze by boat from Canada and Central America. The boats, known as "blacks," corresponded by radio with stations onshore, us-

Mugshot of famous Chicago gangster Al Capone. He profited greatly from the illegal sale of alcohol during Prohibition.

Disposing of Prohibition-era alcohol

ing a variety of codes. "Some of these are of a complexity never even attempted by any government for its most secret communications," wrote Elizebeth Friedman, who now worked for the Coast Guard, intercepting and deciphering the rumrunners' messages.

One convoluted system required the sender to look up the plaintext word in a commercial codebook, write down the code number, add 1,000 to it, look up the result in a *different* commercial codebook, write down the code word for that number, then enchipher the word using a monoalphabetic cipher.

But Mrs. Friedman was nearly as clever a cryptanalyst as her husband. Over a three-year period, she solved some twelve thousand secret messages, enabling the Coast Guard to capture countless "blacks" and completely destroy one of the largest smuggling rings.

An amateur cryptologist in New York, perhaps inspired by Elizebeth Friedman's example, claimed to have uncovered a criminal network that communicated through the seemingly

A Bad Case of Acme

One of the most popular commercial codes of the 1920s and 1930s was the Acme, a one-part nomenclator that substituted code words for one hundred thousand commonly used phrases—and some that it's hard to imagine ever having the opportunity to use. Here are a few of the more amusing (or alarming) examples:

CODE WORD	PLAINTEXT PHRASE
CHOOG	Lard in bladders
GNUEK	Rubber, slightly moldy
BUKSI	Avoid arrest if possible
PYTUO	Collided with an iceberg
HEHST	Clammy condition
OBNYX	Escape at once
CULKE	Bad as can possibly be

innocuous medium of newspaper comic strips. As proof, he offered this sinister plaintext message, deciphered from a Dick Tracy strip: Nero mob in fog rob Leroy apt rat in it are a goy. Writer David Kahn has a term for such misguided attempts to find a cipher where there is none; he calls it *enigmaduction*.

Another example—probably apocryphal—of enigmaduction involves a sign that once hung next to a hitching post outside a country store. It read TOTI EMU LESTO. The townsfolk puzzled over the strange message for days before finally asking the proprietor what it said. As it turned out, the only thing strange about it was the spacing of the letters. Put spaces after the second, fifth, and tenth letters, instead, and the meaning will be clear.

By the mid-1920s, Americans had bigger things to worry about than rumrunning and comic-strip criminals. The Japanese government had signed a treaty with the West, limiting the size of its navy, but Japan was beginning to resent the restrictions. Worried that trouble was brewing, the U.S. military set up a ring of listening posts around the Pacific to monitor Japanese communications.

But Herbert Hoover's election in 1928 dealt a deathblow to the American Black Chamber. Hoover, who promoted peace and international goodwill, was shocked to learn that the government was spying on other countries. His secretary of state closed down the Chamber, declaring indignantly, "Gentlemen should not read each other's mail."

Meanwhile, Japan's Black

Herbert
Hoover
....
American, 1874–1964,
31st President of
the United States

Chamber, the Tokumu Han, was stepping up efforts to break the Gray code used by the United States in Asia. The nomenclator-based system had been in use so long that American diplomats had memorized many of the code words. When the consul at Shanghai retired, he gave his farewell speech in Gray and the audience understood it perfectly. The code finally met its demise after Japanese agents stole discarded telegrams enciphered in Gray from the wastebaskets at the U.S. embassy.

The Tokumu Han was also busy improving its own encryption methods. The Japanese language poses special problems for cryptographers because the traditional written form, *kanji*, isn't based on an English-style alphabet. Like Chinese, it uses ideograms that stand for whole words, phrases, or ideas.

There's also a form of Japanese writing called *kata kana*, which uses phonetic symbols to represent various syllables. As a British codebreaker explains, "Foreign names were normally spelled out in *kana*. Until one got used to them, they were not always easy to recognize: CHI-YA-A-CHI-RU does not obviously spell out 'Churchill' [Britain's prime minister] to the untrained eye."

To send messages by Morse code, the Japanese developed a system called *romaji*, which translates *kana* syllables into Roman letters. One advantage of *romaji* is that it can be enciphered by all the usual methods. It also has one big disadvantage: It's especially vulnerable to frequency analysis. For example, in Romanized Japanese, a *y* is nearly always followed by an *a*, but almost never by an *e* or an *i*, and vowels very often show up in pairs— *oo*, *uu*, *ai*, *ei*, and so on.

Anxious to increase security, Japanese cryptographers developed Enigma-style cipher machines. An early model known as *angoo-ki taipu* A (Type A) featured two electric typewriters with a telephone plug board and a rotor between them. An improved model called, naturally, *angoo-ki taipu* B appeared in 1939. In place of rotors, it had six telephone exchange switches, each with twenty-five contact points. This machine, which American cryptanalysts nicknamed Purple, was the one Japan would use during World War II to encrypt its diplomatic correspondence.

The Germans, meanwhile, were still relying on the thirty thousand Enigmas they'd bought from Arthur Scherbius. "To these two machines," writes historian Ronald Lewin, "the Japanese and the Germans gave their total confidence . . . convinced to the point of self delusion that Purple and Enigma would protect even their most secret signals."

At first their confidence seemed warranted. Britain's

Arthur Scherbius

German, 1878–1929, electrical engineer who designed Germany's Enigma machine

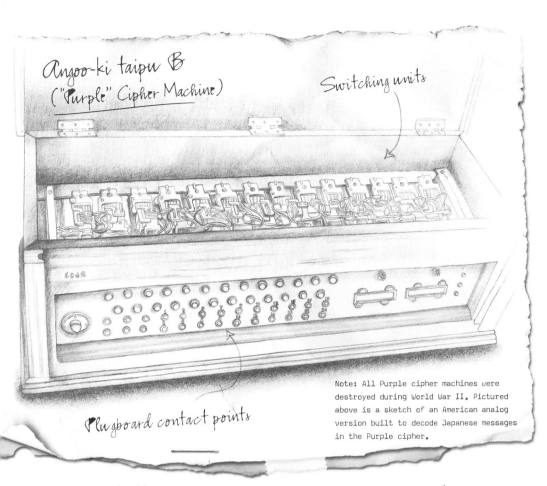

Angoo-ki taipu B
("Purple" Cipher Machine)

Switching units

Plugboard contact points

5042

Note: All Purple cipher machines were destroyed during World War II. Pictured above is a sketch of an American analog version built to decode Japanese messages in the Purple cipher.

Room 40 had been intercepting Enigma messages since 1926 but were having no luck deciphering them. The United States wasn't much help now that the Black Chamber was defunct. Besides, America didn't consider Germany much of a threat.

But Germany's neighbor Poland did feel threatened, and for good reason: German dictator Adolf Hitler was making plans to invade Poland. The Polish cipher bureau, the Biuro Szyfrów, was

URPDQFH, UXP, DQG URPDML

One of only three surviving pieces of a Purple machine. This photo shows a part of the interior switching unit that electronically converted plaintext to the Purple cipher.

so desperate to read Germany's Enigma-enciphered messages that it hired a psychic to try to make sense of them.

Then, in 1931, the Biuro had a stroke of luck when it obtained a set of instruction books for the Enigma. With the help of a team of mathematicians, the Biuro built its own version of the Enigma. In August 1939, two weeks before the German invasion, the Poles smuggled the replica into England.

Armed with knowledge of the Enigma's inner workings, the British Code and Cipher School at Bletchley Park—the successor to Room 40—launched a new assault on Germany's ciphers.

The Turing Bombe (above) was used by British cryptanyalists to help decipher Enigma messages.

CHAPTER THIRTEEN

Hounds, Magicians, and Indians

1939 CE – 1945 CE

Bletchley Park (above) was home to the British Code and Cipher School.

One supervisor at Bletchley Park described his cryptanalysts as "a pack of hounds trying to pick up the scent." According to Simon Singh, they were "a bizarre combination of mathematicians, scientists, linguists, classicists, chess grandmasters and crossword addicts." New recruits had to demonstrate their skills by completing the London *Daily Telegraph*'s challenging crossword in twelve minutes or less.

Naturally, German cryptanalysts were trying just as hard to decipher Britain's military messages. But the British had one big advantage: They realized that their own encipherment methods were vulnerable, and regularly changed them. The Germans, on

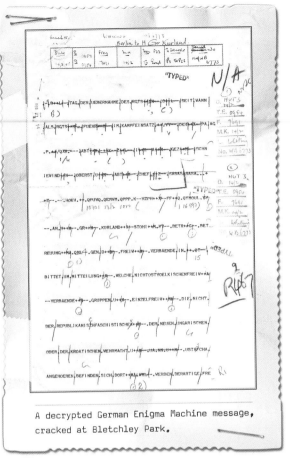

A decrypted German Enigma Machine message, cracked at Bletchley Park.

the other hand, considered their system totally secure. But, says historian Peter Calvocoressi, "Engima was unbreakable only if the Germans always kept to the rules—which, being human, they would not." The machine's operators made several common mistakes that, though they were small, provided a crack through which Bletchley Park's codebreakers could attack the system.

As Kerckhoffs's principle points out, knowing how a cipher machine works isn't enough; you have to know what key the operator is using. The Germans prefaced each message with a three-letter key that changed daily; it told the receiver how to set the rotors. The key letters were supposed to be totally random, but in the heat of battle operators often chose three consecutive letters on the Enigma keyboard, or used the same key repeatedly. British cryptanalysts called these predictable keys *cillies*.

In addition, the messages themselves contained standard

words and phrases. For example, each morning the Germans broadcast an enciphered weather report; the word *wetter* (weather) almost invariably appeared, usually in the same position. A word or phrase like this, whose plaintext equivalent can be easily guessed, is called a *crib*.

Thanks in part to cribs and cillies, Bletchley Park became more and more adept at reading the Enigma cipher; the information they gleaned was used by British forces to locate and sink enemy tankers and supply ships. But the Germans still wouldn't accept the possibility that their code had been cracked.

The unraveling of Enigma was a major factor in Germany's defeat. General Eisenhower (later president) wrote, "It has saved thousands of British and American lives and, in no small way, contributed to the speed with which the enemy was routed." One British historian believes that "the war, instead of finishing in 1945, would have ended in 1948 had the Government Code and Cypher School not been able to read the Engima cyphers."

While Bletchley Park was struggling with Enigma, American cryptographers were puzzling over

This World War II photo shows General Dwight D. Eisenhower speaking to troops before D-Day.

William Friedman at work on a cipher machine.

the ciphers that Germany's ally Japan was creating with the Engima-style machine known as Purple.

After the American Black Chamber folded, the military's Signal Intelligence Service took over the job of monitoring foreign communications. The head of SIS's cryptological branch was our old friend William Friedman. Before the United States entered the war, Friedman could afford only a small staff, whom he called "magicians," and had very limited resources. "All we had," recalled one of the cryptanalysts, "was pen and paper and a calculator."

When Japan introduced the Purple cipher in 1939, the magicians set to work on it it, using methods similar to Bletchley Park's. Purple's workings were even more complex than Enigma's. "Apparently," wrote Friedman, "the machine had with malicious intent—but brilliantly—been constructed to suppress all plain-text repetition." After a year and a half of trial and error, the team deduced how the device was wired and built a replica.

Exhausted by the effort, Friedman had a nervous breakdown and was given a less taxing assignment. But he was far from finished with cryptology; he devoted much of his spare time to that still-unsolved puzzle, the Voynich manuscript. The only insight Friedman could offer was that the strange writing must

The U.S.S. California sinking during the attack on Pearl Harbor.

be some sort of artificial language.

America, which had been largely ignoring developments in the rest of the world, soon came to regret its isolationist tendencies. On December 7, 1941, Japan attacked Pearl Harbor, plunging the United States headlong into the war. Overnight, military intelligence became a top priority.

The SIS could now decipher messages sent in Purple, but that was used only for Japan's diplomatic correspondence. The Japanese navy, unable to afford the expensive cipher machines, relied on a nomenclator system known as JN25, which substituted five-digit code numbers for over thirty thousand words, phrases, and syllables—not a very secure method, if that had been the extent of it. But the code numbers were enciphered by subtracting another five-digit number from them, *then* the resulting number was encoded by indicating on what page, column, and line of the codebook it appeared!

Luckily, Japanese radio operators committed the same error as their German counterparts —they used predictable patterns of words and phrases. Before long, American cryptanalysts were deciphering large chunks of the Japanese navy's transmissions.

But they couldn't quite figure out the codes used to designate various Pacific islands and ports, such as **AK** for Pearl Harbor.

In May 1942, Japan was planning a major attack on a location identified only as **AF**. SIS codebreakers suspected that **AF** was Midway Island. To test this hypothesis, American naval officers hatched a clever scheme. Using a secure underwater cable, they instructed the radio operator at Midway to send out a plaintext message saying that the island's freshwater distilling plant had broken down.

Just as they hoped, the transmission was intercepted by Japanese operators, who reported to headquarters that **AF** was short on fresh water—confirming that the letters stood for Midway. When Japanese ships descended on the island, they found a fleet of enemy destroyers and aircraft carriers waiting for them.

The Allied victory at Midway was a turning point of the war. "Had we lacked early information of the Japanese movements," said American admiral Chester Nimitz, ". . . the Battle of Midway would have ended differently."

The Americans couldn't be content with breaking the enemy's codes and ciphers, of course; they needed a secure system of their own. In the decade before the war, the navy had developed a cipher machine similar to Enigma, but with one significant difference—the rotors didn't advance in a predictable sequence like those in the Enigma, so the enciphering process was even more complex. During the war, both the army and navy used an improved version, which they dubbed SIGABA. Neither the Germans nor the Japanese managed to crack it.

Photo of an American SIGABA Cipher machine.

Though World War II introduced what writer Francis Russell calls "a bewildering arsenal of communications devices," the old, low-tech methods of cryptography were not suddenly obsolete. A German spy captured in 1942 carried a handkerchief with a message in invisible ink made from copper sulfate. When the FBI exposed the cloth to ammonia fumes, it revealed the names and addresses of seven other spies.

Nazi agents in England once sent a report to Germany by means of an ingenious semagram (a message that uses neither numbers or letters) in the form of a knitted sweater. The yarn contained a series of small knots; when it was unraveled and held up alongside an alphabet of a specified length, the position of the knots indicated the plaintext letters.

Political prisoners inside Germany used a steganographic technique similar to the old ball-of-wax trick from ancient China: They wrote in minuscule letters on one-inch squares of toilet paper, then tucked them inside the tags of their worn-out shirts, which were collected by Red Cross workers when they brought new clothing.

The most successful trench code of World War II was a throw-back to the first century BCE, when Roman officers in Britain wrote their dispatches in a language the enemy didn't know. But the secret language adopted by American forces wasn't Greek. It was Navajo.

During World War I, both the United States and Canada had considered using Native American languages as a form of spoken code. The Americans even put a few code talkers from the Choctaw, Comanche, Osage, Cheyenne, and Sioux nations on the front lines in France. But when the war ended, so did the experiment.

It was resurrected in 1942 by Philip Johnston, a white missionary's son who grew up on a Navajo reservation. By the age of

nine, Johnston had become so fluent in the language that, when a delegation of Navajos went to Washington to meet with President Theodore Roosevelt, they took the boy along as a translator.

Native American languages weren't as alien to Europeans as you might expect. Large numbers of German students,

Navajo code talkers in the field during World War II.

The Curious Case of the Coded Crosswords

In May 1944, shortly before the Allies invaded Europe, the London *Daily Telegraph* printed a series of alarming crossword puzzles. The first two contained the words **Utah** and **Omaha**—code names for the beaches where Allied forces would land. The next had the word **overlord**—the military's name for the entire invasion plan. Then the word **mulberry** appeared—the code name for the floating harbors that were to be towed across the English Channel. The last puzzle, published just four days before the D-Day invasion, featured the word **Neptune**—the navy's code word for its operations. Clearly, as Allied agents feared, the crosswords were devised by Nazi spies.

Or not. As far as British intelligence could determine, the whole thing was just an incredible coincidence, another example of enigmaduction.

fascinated by the American West, had visited reservations and studied Indian dialects. But the Navajos were so isolated and their language was so difficult to master that they had been largely ignored.

Johnston convinced the Marine Corps to take on twenty-

Several Native American tribes were recruited as code talkers. Pictured above are the Comanche of the US Army 4th Signal Division.

nine Navajo recruits, some as young as fifteen, to be trained as code talkers. There was one major problem, though: Battlefield jargon was full of words that had no equivalent in Navajo. The code talkers' first task was to devise a nomenclator that substituted Navajo words for military terms. "Commanding officer" became "war chief." A mortar was a "gun that squats." Ships were given the names of fish—a battleship was a whale, a destroyer was a shark. Planes were named after birds—a dive-bomber was a chicken hawk, bombs were eggs.

The recruits also provided substitutes for the letters of the English alphabet so terms that weren't on the nomenclator could be spelled out. For the letter A, they used the Navajo word for "ant," **wol-la-chee**; B was "bear," or **shush**; C was "cat," or **moasi**, and so on.

The first code talkers who went overseas had more to worry about than remembering the code words. When regular radio operators in the Pacific theater began getting messages in an unfamiliar language, they assumed their outposts had been captured by the Japanese. Even worse, the Navajos, who tended to be small and dark-skinned, were sometimes mistaken for the enemy and taken prisoner.

There was skepticism about the code's usefulness, too. One code talker described his commander's attitude:

An American M-209 Cipher machine.

> He said he would keep us on one condition: that I could out-race his "white code"—a mechanical ticking cylinder thing [probably the M-209, a small Engima-style machine]. We both sent messages, by white cylinder and by my voice. Both of us received answers and the race was to see who could decode his answer first. . . . The other guy was still decoding when I got the roger on my return message in about four and a half minutes. I said, "Colonel, when are you going to give up on that cylinder thing?"

Eventually the code talkers numbered over four hundred. During the crucial invasion of Iwo Jima, they really proved their worth. In the first two days of battle, they transmitted more than eight hundred messages without a single error and totally baffled Japanese codebreakers. "Were it not for the Navajo code talkers," said one American officer, "the Marines never would have taken Iwo Jima."

CHAPTER FOURTEEN

Bookies, Spies, and POWs

1945 CE – 1974 CE

Though cryptology had become an indispensable military tool, it hadn't lost its appeal as a source of harmless fun. While their fathers were fighting in Europe and the Pacific—and, a few years later, in Korea—thousands of American kids were glued to their radio sets, thrilling to the adventures of Orphan Annie and Captain Midnight and to *Tales of the Texas Rangers.*

All three shows were sponsored by the drink mix Ovaltine. Listeners who sent in enough proofs of purchase received a decoder ring or badge; the devices bore such evocative names as the Sliding Secret Compartment Ring, the Mystic Eye Detector ring, and the Code-O-Graph.

This *Captian Midnight* decoder badge uses an Alberti Disk to decipher messages.

Most were variations of the Alberti disk, with an outer ring of letters and an inner ring of numbers. At the end of each episode, the host read off a string of numbers. The lucky listener who had a decoder could translate the cipher into plaintext. Some messages gave hints about upcoming episodes; others were blatant reminders to drink more Ovaltine.

When Prohibition ended back in 1933, it had put the rumrunners out of business. But the underworld found plenty of other uses for codes and ciphers. Bookmakers conducted what's known as a numbers racket—an illegal version of today's lottery—in which a bettor placed money on a particular three-digit number. To keep his transactions secret, one New York bookie disguised the numbers as musical notes on a bogus piece of sheet music—an **E** note was 1, an **F** was 2, and so on.

Another numbers racketeer recorded his bets in a simple form of shorthand. Others used Greek or Hebrew or even ancient Phoenician letters. A bookie raised in French West Africa wrote down the French word for each number in a crude phonetic form: For example, **SINKKATYUNDEYO** stood for *cinq quatre un deux zéro*, or 54120.

By the 1950s, the United States and its WWII ally, the Soviet Union, were locked in a struggle for economic, political, and military superiority. This so-called Cold War was waged not by

ERRNLHV, VSLHV, DQG SRZV

soldiers but by spies, and cryptography was a secret agent's best defense.

Since most agents couldn't lug around an Engima or SIGABA machine, they relied heavily on a new form of steganography—the microdot. Microphotography had been in use since the Civil War, but in the 1920s German scientists refined the art so that whole pages of information could be contained in a dot .05 inches in diameter.

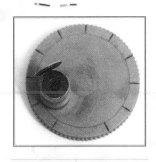

Pictured above is a Mark IV CIA microdot camera. Small enough to be hidden and used in the field, it can produce a microdot 1mm in diameter.

During World War II, a British lab technician examining a letter taken from a German spy noticed that one of the typewritten periods was suspiciously shiny; it was a microdot, of course. Soon, postal censors were finding more microdots in the text of letters or hidden beneath postage stamps. After the war, Soviet agents adopted the new technology, concealing the dots in magazine bindings, in hollow flashlight batteries, even inside fake coins.

The CIA used hollow coins to conceal microdots and other secret objects.

Russia's ultimate cryptological weapon, though, was one that originated in America but never caught on there—the one-time pad. Instead of blocks of letters, the Soviet system—called *gamma*—used random numbers. Using a simple substitution cipher, senders converted the plaintext into five-digit numbers; to these they added the random numbers from the pad, creating an unbreakable cipher. Since the pads were only an inch square, they were easily hidden, and they were made from highly flammable cellulose-nitrate film, so a spy in danger of being caught could burn the evidence.

A One-Time Pad

By the 1960s, the United States was involved in yet another armed conflict, this time in Southeast Asia. American prisoners of war in Vietnam revived a classic cryptographic method, the knock code, basing it on a grid almost identical to the one invented twenty-two centuries earlier by Polybius. Like correspondents today using text messaging or Internet chat rooms, the POWs developed a lexicon of abbreviations; for example, "good morning" became **GM** and "says" was simply **Z**.

One Viet Cong prison camp tried to undermine morale by playing an antiwar message from a famous American folksinger over the loudspeaker. The POWs responded by passing around a message in knock code similar to this: **24 34 11 33 12 11 15 55 43 45 13 25 43**.[*] To decipher it, consult the Polybius square on page 11.

ERRNLHV, VSLHV, DQG SRZV

* Joan Baez sucks.

Captain Jeremiah Denton speaking at Clark Air Base, in the Philippines, after his release as a POW in 1973.

Navy pilot Jeremiah Denton (later a U.S. senator) was held prisoner for seven years by the North Vietnamese, who coerced him into reading an anti-American statement on television. As he stared into the TV camera, Denton blinked rapidly, seemingly bothered by the bright lighting. But U.S. intelligence officers realized there was a pattern to the blinks—Denton was using Morse code to reveal just what sort of coercion the enemy used: **T-O-R-T-U-R-E**.

Ordinarily, of course, the codes the armed forces used were a bit more sophisticated. Even so, military cryptography hadn't made much progress since the 1930s. The most common cipher system in use during the Vietnam War was an improved version of the Engima-style rotor machine.

But new technology was being developed that would make the earthshaking effects of the telegraph and the radio look like insignificant tremors.

CHAPTER FIFTEEN

Colossus, Lucifer, and *Kryptos*

1945 CE – Present

Not counting Charles Babbage's difference engine—which never got much past the design stage—the first device that could really be called a computer was a colossal machine appropriately named Colossus. It was created in the 1940s by Britain's Bletchley Park to crack a German system called the Lorenz cipher. Colossus could read five thousand characters per second and, like today's computers, was programmable.

After the war, British intelligence was afraid the device might fall into the wrong hands and so ordered the plans and the Colossus itself destroyed. For decades afterward, credit for inventing the computer was given to two University of Pennsylvania scientists who, in 1945, had built another hulk-

The Colossus computer

ing device called the Electronic Numerical Integrator and Calculator or ENIAC.

Computers have, of course, transformed once again the way we communicate. Their impact on cryptography has been even more profound. Traditional methods of encryption can't hope to withstand cryptanalysis by computer. What chance does a Vigenère cipher or Alberti disk or even an Engima machine have against a mathematical marvel that performs thousands of calculations per second?

But, as cryptologist Albrecht Beutelspacher points out, "not only is the computer the cause of a great many problems, it is, ironically, also the key to their solution." If computers are good at cracking ciphers, they're just as good at creating them.

By the 1960s, computers were so small and so affordable that businesses were using them to keep transactions confidential. The problem was, each company had its own method of encryption, which made it tough to communicate with other companies.

Finally, in 1976, America's National Bureau of Standards adopted a process called Luci-

ENIAC (pictured above) weighed 30 tons and measured 8.5 feet x 3 feet x 80 feet.

fer. In simple terms, the system turns plaintext into a string of ones and zeros, encrypts those using a complex substitution method, then scrambles them repeatedly. The Lucifer cipher became the country's first official Data Encryption Standard (DES). Problem solved.

The above computer, called COPACABANA, was built in 2005 by Bochum and Kiel Universities in Germany. It is designed to peform millions of calculations necessary to crack a DES system.

Well, almost. There was still one little glitch. Like the Vigenère system, DES needs a key—in this case, a number—to tell it exactly how to encrypt the message. Obviously, the receiver has to know the key in order to read the message. So the question is, how does the sender pass the key on to the receiver without revealing it to anybody else?

At first, businesses sent the keys by courier, but that got complicated and expensive. DES is called a *symmetric* system because it uses a single key known to both sender and receiver. What large corporations needed was an *asymmetric* system, which uses one key to encipher the message and a different one to decipher it. The enciphering key can be a *public key*, available to anyone, as long as the deciphering key is known only to the receiver.

An asymmetric system is often compared to a padlock: Anybody can lock it, but only someone with the right key or the

Clifford
Cocks
....
American, 1950–,
inventor of Public-
Key cryptography

right combination can unlock it. A process like this, one that's easy to do but difficult to undo, is called a *one-way function*.

In 1973, Britain's Government Communications Headquarters—the successor to Bletchley Park—asked mathematician Clifford Cocks to devise a really secure set of keys. Cocks later wrote:

> *Because I had been working in number theory, it was natural to think about one-way functions . . . From start to finish, it took me no more than half an hour. I was quite pleased with myself. I thought, "Ooh, that's nice. I've been given a problem and I've solved it."*

His "nice" solution would prove to be what code expert Simon Singh calls "the greatest cryptographic achievement since the invention of the monoalphabetic cipher." Cocks had discovered that a relatively simple mathematical process called *factoring* can create a two-key encryption system that is, for all practical purposes, unbreakable. For more details about how the process works, see the sidebar.

a One-Way Trip to Secureville

Life is full of one-way functions. It's easy to squeeze toothpaste out of a tube, but a lot tougher to put it back. You can mix several hues of paint to make a new color, but try unmixing them. It took only a minor fall to break Humpty Dumpty, but all the king's men couldn't patch him up. (One-way functions are sometimes called Humpty-Dumpty functions.)

Basic math is mostly a two-way street. It's easy to add 3 and 4 to get 7, and just as easy to subtract 4 from 7 and get 3; it's no harder to divide 10 by 2 and get 5 than it is to multiply 5 and 2 and get 10.

But factoring is a little trickier. Briefly, here's how it works: Start with two prime numbers—11 and 13, for example. (A prime number can be divided only by itself or by 1.) Multiply them and you get a *composite number*: 143.

A factoring problem starts out by giving you a composite number. You have to determine what two prime numbers (or factors) can be multiplied to make that number. A small number like 143 can be factored easily by trial and error. But what if the composite number has hundreds of digits?

A high-speed computer can do the job, of course—eventually. In 1994, researchers at Oregon State University started with this number:

22196205286597019526601207430761004273909243570733965516770339373353207430502358024273032756332005408066894606696792219545093967127330845624462896060302682123117

They found it was the product of

16537237851564688924261407041648853990657743

muliplied by

4971867800323378818776339900596001648747659834953921156974700575915322824191116704320092701688428573103024883134912419

Using thirty computer stations, the task took them eight weeks.

Now let's see how factoring is used in encryption. Suppose two colleagues—in keeping with cryptological tradition, we'll call them Bob and Alice—want to exchange confidential information. For his private key, Bob chooses two prime numbers, which he multiplies to get a composite number—the

public key. He gives Alice only the public
key. She uses it to encrypt her messages to
him by means of a complicated process that
can be reversed only with the private key.
Technically, of course, Bob and Alice's
competition could figure out the private key
by factoring the public one. But by the time
they succeed, Bob will be using a new key.

Remember how Babbage got no credit for breaking the Vigenère cipher because British intelligence didn't want its enemies
to know about it? Remember how Colossus sank into obscurity
because British intelligence didn't want its enemies to know
about it? Then you can guess what happened to Clifford Cocks
and his brilliant breakthrough.

In 1976, three American cryptographers, unaware of Cocks's
work, introduced the concept of public-key cryptography; the
following year, three researchers at Massachusetts Institute of
Technology came up with a practical method of implementing
the idea. They christened it RSA—the first letters of their last
names. It was essentially the same as Cocks's method.

Because RSA is more complex and slower than DES, it's been
used mainly for messages that require a high level of security.
In 2000, the National Institute of Standards and Technology

(formerly the National Bureau of Standards) replaced the aging DES with a stronger encryption algorithm called AES. Already there are doubts about whether the latest cipher can withstand an assault by tomorrow's breed of computers. These machines will likely use the principles of quantum mechanics (which are too complicated to explain, even in a sidebar) to perform tasks far faster than conventional computers.

"If quantum computers become a reality," says engineering professor John Rarity, "the whole game changes." Cryptographers aren't waiting until that happens to prepare a defense. Several laboratories have already developed enciphering systems based on quantum mechanics.

• • •   • — — •   • —   — • — •   •

According to Phil Zimmermann, inventor of a nonquantum system called Pretty Good Privacy, "It is now possible to make ciphers . . . that are really, really out of reach of all known forms of cryptanalysis. And I think it's going to stay that way."

But of course people once considered the Vigenère system and the Engima machine unbreakable. No matter how sophisticated an enciphering method is, sooner or later it's almost sure to be compromised, either by human error or by human ingenuity or treachery. And, says a computer expert at MIT, "There's nothing quantum mechanics can do about that."

Still, Zimmerman may be right. Maybe it *is* possible to create an unbreakable cipher. And maybe you don't have to use quantum mechanics to do it. After all, there are a number of cryptograms kicking around that, even though they

Phil
Zimmermann
....
American, 1954–,
author of the Pretty
Good Privacy (PGP)
program

were created by centuries-old methods, have yet to be broken.

The most durable, of course, is the Voynich manuscript, which is still a subject of cryptographic contention. Philologist John Stojko claims that the book's strange script is a form of Ukrainian, and that he has deciphered such profound messages as this: "Emptiness is that what Baby God's Eye is fighting for." Gordon Rugg, a British university professor, suspects the manuscript is a fake, concocted by Elizabethan forger and con man Edward Kelley to bilk the original buyer, Rudolph II. He says Kelley could have created a nonsense text by using a variation of the Cardano grille. But these are only theories.

Though there's an entire organization devoted to cracking the Beale Cipher and recovering the treasure, the cipher page that reveals the whereabouts of the treasure continues to defy solution. There are a number of other celebrated cryptograms that remain unsolved, including one devised by the famous English

FRORVVXV, OXFLIHU, DQG NUBSWRV

composer Edward Elgar. Elgar's "Dorabella" cipher dates back to 1897, the Beale Cipher to 1885 or before, and the Voynich to at least the seventeenth century.

The fact that all of these unsolved puzzles are over a century old doesn't mean that the art of making crack-resistant ciphers is lost. A stone, wood, and metal sculpture titled *Kryptos* stands in front of CIA headquarters in Langley, Virginia. Created by artist James Sanborn, it features an S-shaped copper screen with four lengthy substitution ciphers carved into it. Since the building opened in 1991, three of the four ciphers have succumbed to cryptanalysis. The fourth remains an enigma. But who knows how much longer it, or the others, will hold out? If you want to be the first to solve them, you'd better get busy.

The Kryptos sculpture at CIA headquarters remains unsolved.

?OBKRUOXOGHULBSOLIFBBWFLRVQQPRNGKSSOTWTQSJQSSEKZZ
WATJKLUDIAWINFBNYPVTTMZFPKWGDKZXTJCDIGKUHUAUEKCAR

Page 4, "At a time": Innes, Brian. *The Book of Spies: 4000 Years of Cloak & Dagger*, p. 12.

Page 6, "since the danger": Rawlinson, George, trans. *Herodotus: The Persian Wars*, p. 594.

Page 13, "I wrote the": Wiseman, Anne and Peter, trans. *The Battle for Gaul* by Julius Caesar, p. 109.

Page 14, "he changed the": Beutelspacher, Albrecht. *Cryptology*, p. 5.

Page 15, "A letter . . . escapes": Kahn, David. *The Codebreakers*, p. 774.

Page 16, "in the most": Machiavelli, Niccolò. *The Art of War*, Ch. 7.

Page 20, "no Irish scholar" and "such of our": Kahn, p. 90.

Page 21, "A man is": Bacon, Roger. *Roger Bacon on the Nullity of Magic*, pp. 39-40.

Page 22, "When you want": Kahn, pp. 97-98.

Page 27, "The growth of": Kahn, p. 108.

Page 28, "the most significant": Singh, Simon. *The Code Book*: p. 46.

Page 28, "I make two": Kahn, p. 127.

Page 29, "not in regular": Kahn, p. 128.

Page 36, "a thoroughgoing knave": Newton, David E. *Encyclopedia of Cryptology*, p. 43.

Page 39, "the archetypal system": Kahn, p. 145.

Page 41, "the longer the": Kahn, p. 150.

Page 44, "The key cipher": Kahn, p. 150.

Page 47, "Myself with ten": Singh, p. 37.

Page 49, "writing always on": Guy, John. *Queen of Scots: The True Life of Mary Stuart*, p. 465.

Page 49, "The affairs being": Guy, p. 468.

Page 49, "bowelled alive and": Singh, p. 42.

Page 50, "A weak encryption": Singh, p. 41.

Page 51, "somewhat tedious": Beutelspacher, p. 5.

Page 51, "the confederate with": Kahn, p. 150.

Page 57, "Worthie Sir John": Wrixon, Fred B. *Codes, Ciphers & Other Cryptic & Clandestine Communications*, p. 494.

Page 62, "Not having at hand": Kahn, p. 616.

Page 64, "owe the Esteem": Kahn, p. 173.

Page 68, "the maiden Name": Weber, Ralph E. *United States Diplomatic Codes and Ciphers: 1775-1938*, p. 35.

Page 68, "I know very": Weber, p. 31.

Page 68, "is no[t] adept" and "I hate a cipher": Weber, p. 30.

Page 72, "Three Numbers make": Kahn, p. 177.

Page 73, "What was my": Weber, p. 103.

Page 83, "Half-a-dozen people": Kahn, p. 189.

Page 83, "it is easy": Kahn, pp. 783-784.

Page 84, "Letters were poured": Poe, Edgar Allan. *Essays and Reviews*, p. 1281.

Page 84, "human ingenuity cannot": Poe, *Essays and Reviews*, p. 1278.

Page 85, "the most profound": Kahn, p. 786.

Page 86, "A good glass": Harrison, James A., ed. *The Complete Works of Edgar Allan Poe*, p. 119.

Page 89, "The bigger boys": Singh, p. 66.

Page 94, "a system is": Ball, W. W. Rouse. *Mathematical Recreations & Essays*, p. 408.

Page 96, "metal buttons, which": Markle, Donald E. *Spies and Spymasters of the Civil War*, pp. 35-36.

Page 99, "It was on": Kahn, pp. 862-863.

Page 101, "from fifteen to twenty": Weber, p. 219.

Page 101, "the most bitterly": Wrixon, p. 64.

Page 102, "Few false ideas": Kahn, p. 763.

Page 103, "The security of": Newton, *Encyclopedia of Cryptology*, p. 155.

Page 105, "Dear Charlie, Write": Singh, p. 80.

Page 106, "Descend into the": Verne, Jules.

A Journey to the Center of the Earth, Ch. 3.

Page 106, "fairly familiar with": Conan
   Doyle, A. *The Complete Sherlock Holmes,*
   pp. 606-607.

Page 106, "There are many": Conan Doyle,
   pp. 904-905.

Page 107, "one of those" and "The supply of":
   Conan Doyle, p. 436.

Page 108, "to avoid the": Singh, p. 86.

Page 109, "With this idea": Singh, p. 90.

Page 110, "reduced from comparative," "resolved to sever," and "determined to make":
   Singh, p. 93.

Page 110, "to devote only": Singh, p. 98.

Page 112, "perhaps the most": Norman,
   Bruce. *Secret Warfare: The Battle of Codes
   and Ciphers,* p. 49.

Page 114, "I cannot deny": Kahn, p. 297.

Page 115, "There certainly never": Kahn, p. 331.

Page 115, "the Holy Grail": Singh, p. 122.

Page 117, "permanent organization": Kahn,
   p. 355.

Page 117, "sees all, hears all": Singh, p. 138.

Page 117, "the most mysterious": *Mysteries of
   Mind, Space & Time: The Unexplained,* p. 3065.

Page 118, "a bizarre mixture": Lewin, Ronald.
*The American Magic: Codes, Ciphers, and the
Defeat of Japan,* p. 81.

Page 118, "book containing" and "bestowed
   much time": Kahn, p. 866.

Page 119, "a victim of": *Mysteries of Mind,
   Space & Time,* p. 3068.

Page 120, "The natural inquisitiveness":
   Russell, Francis and the Editors of
   Time-Life Books. *The Secret War,* p. 68.

Page 124, "a fairly regular" and "curiously
   jumbled groups": *Mysteries of Mind, Space
   & Time,* p. 1048.

Page 125, "I thought him": Kahn, p. 948.

Page 125, "Neither I nor": Kahn, p. 887.

Page 128, "Some of these": Kahn, p. 804.

Page 130, "Gentlemen should not": Singh, p. 141.

Page 131, "Foreign names were": Smith,
   Michael. *The Emperor's Codes: The
   Breaking of Japan's Secret Ciphers,* p. 160.

Page 132, "To these two": Lewin, *The
   American Magic,* p. 36.

Page 135, "a pack of hounds" and "a bizzare
   combination": Singh, p. 165.

Page 136, "Enigma was unbreakable":
   Calvocoressi, Peter. *Top Secret Ultra,* p. 49.

Page 137, "It has saved": Winterbotham, F.
   W. *The Ultra Secret,* p. 3.

Page 137, "the war, instead": Singh, p. 187.

Page 138, "All we had": Smith, *The Emperor's
   Codes,* p. 69.

Page 138, "Apparently the machine": Smith,
   The Emperor's Codes, p. 71.

Page 140, "Had we lacked": Norman, *Secret
   Warfare,* p. 66.

Page 141, "a bewildering arsenal": Norman,
   Secret Warfare, p. 57.

Page 145, "He said he": Singh, p. 198.

Page 145, "Were it not": Aaseng, Nathan.
   Navajo Code Talkers, p. 99.

Page 152, "not only is": Beutelspacher,
   Cryptology, p. ix.

Page 154, "Because I had": Singh, pp. 284-285.

Page 154, "the greatest cryptographic": Singh,
   p. 252.

Page 158, "If quantum computers": Stix,
   Gary. "Best-kept Secrets." *Scientific
   American,* January 2005, p. 78.

Page 158, "It is now": Singh, p. 317.

Page 158, "There's nothing quantum": Stix,
   "Best-kept Secrets," p. 84.

Page 159, "Emptiness is that": Rugg, G.
   "The Mystery of the Voynich Manuscript." *Scientific American,* July 2004,
   p 106.

algorithm   The procedure (Cardano grille, rail fence, Caesar cipher, etc.) that is used to encipher or decipher a secret message.

bookie or **bookmaker**   A person who handles wagers made by individual bettors, usually on horse races or other sporting events.

Caesar, Gaius Julius   (100-44 BCE) Roman general who became dictator of Rome in 49 BCE. He was murdered by several former allies who feared he was becoming too powerful.

ciphertext   The symbols, letters, or numbers that make up a cryptogram.

cryptogram   A secret message written using a code or cipher.

Elizabeth I   (1533-1603) Queen of England who took the throne at the age of twenty-five after the death of her half sister, Mary I. She ruled for forty-five years.

factoring   A mathematical process for determining what two numbers, or factors, can be multiplied to make a composite number.

frequency analysis   A technique for cracking a cipher by replacing the most common letters in the ciphertext with the most frequently used letters in the ordinary alphabet.

key   A tool for creating a polyalphabetic cipher. The keyword or number indicates which alphabet is used to encipher each letter of the plaintext.

Mary, Queen of Scots   (1542-1587) Daughter of King James V of Scotland. When she was six days old her father died and Mary became nominal queen of Scotland. Many considered her the rightful heir to the English throne because the marriage of Elizabeth's mother to Henry VIII hadn't been recognized by the Catholic Church.

monoalphabetic cipher   A system in which a given plaintext letter is always enciphered by the same ciphertext letter or symbol.

nomenclator   A list of code words or numbers that can be substituted for plaintext words and phrases.

null A number, letter, or symbol that's not part of the text, but is inserted only to make the cipher harder to solve.

one-time pad A system in which the sender uses as the key a set of random letters or numbers printed on a pad. If the letters or numbers are truly random, you can't break the cipher—unless you have a copy of the pad and know which page to use.

one-way function A process, usually a mathematical one, that can be performed far more easily in one direction than in the other.

plaintext The original wording of a message, before it's enciphered. Also called *cleartext*.

Poe, Edgar Allan (1809-1849) American short story writer, poet, and critic, best known for his detective stories ("The Murders in the Rue Morgue") and eerie tales ("The Tell-Tale Heart," "The Pit and the Pendulum").

polyalphabetic cipher A enciphering method that has more than one possible substitute for each letter of the plaintext.

Prohibition A period from 1920-1933 when the manufacture and sale of alcoholic beverages was outlawed by the Eighteenth Amendment to the United States Constitution.

steganography A means of sending a message secretly by concealing it rather than enciphering it.

substitution cipher One of the two basic types of ciphers. As the name implies, each letter of the plaintext is replaced with a substitute letter or number. A simple example is the Caesar cipher.

transposition cipher The other basic type of cipher. It uses the original letters of the plaintext, but rearranges, or transposes, them. One example is the rail fence cipher.

Aaseng, Nathan. *Navajo Code Talkers*. New York: Walker, 1992.
Aimed at young readers, Aaseng's book not only shows how the Navajo code worked, it recounts the shabby treatment Navajos suffered before, during, and after the war.

Butler, William S. and L. Douglas Keeney. *Secret Messages: Concealment, Codes, and Other Types of Ingenious Communication*. New York: Simon & Schuster, 2001.
An entertaining and wide-ranging collection of anecdotes about codes and ciphers.

Kahn, David. *The Codebreakers: The Story of Secret Writing*. New York: Macmillan, 1967.
The first comprehensive study of cryptology, and, though it's a little outdated, still the best.

Newton, David E. *Encyclopedia of Cryptology*. Santa Barbara, CA: ABC-Clio, 1997.
A useful reference work with succinct but fairly detailed entries on all aspects of the art.

Singh, Simon. *The Code Book: The Evolution of Secrecy from Mary Queen of Scots to Quantum Cryptography*. New York: Doubleday, 1999.
A very readable and thorough history of cryptology that, contrary to what the title implies, takes us all the way back to ancient Greece.

Weber, Ralph E. *United States Diplomatic Codes and Ciphers: 1775-1938*. Chicago: Precedent, 1979.
A fascinating in-depth look at how the art of diplomacy and the art of cryptography developed simultaneously.

Wrixon, Fred B. *Codes, Ciphers & Other Cryptic & Clandestine Communications: Making and Breaking Secret Messages from Hieroglyphs to the Internet*. New York: Barnes & Noble, 1998.
Seven hundred pages of information on every conceivable type of code and cipher, with loads of diagrams and illustrations, plus a lengthy section of cryptograms for the reader to solve.

· TO LEARN MORE ABOUT ·
CODES AND CIPHERS

Fiction

Bruchac, Joseph. *Code Talker: A Novel About the Navajo Marines of World War Two.* New York: Puffin, 2006.

This well-written, well-researched young-adult novel promotes respect for Native American culture as it follows protagonist Ned Begay from his early years in an English school to his experiences on the battlefield.

Hicks, Clifford B. *Alvin's Secret Code.* New York: Puffin, 1998.

Part of a classic children's series first published over thirty years ago, now back in print. Twelve-year-old Alvin Fernald and his best friend use codes and ciphers to solve a mystery.

Nonfiction

Singh, Simon. *The Code Book: How to Make it, Break It, Hack It, Crack It.* New York: Delacorte, 2002.

A somewhat simpler and more accessible (but not dumbed-down) version of Singh's best-selling adult title, *The Code Book.*

Online

www.secretcodebreaker.com/codes.html

A multitude of ciphers you can make or break, from the Caesar to the autokey.

www.voynich.nu

An extensive site devoted to the "most mysterious manuscript in the world," including a detailed description of the book's contents and the efforts that have been made to decipher it.

www.ariplex.com/tina/tbeale05.htm

The complete text of the Beale papers, plus an analysis and a demonstration of how the Declaration of Independence works as a key.

LQGHA

A CKED
..ter 1-8-58
..rton, State Dept.
By *Mark A Eckhoff Archivist*
Date *Oct. 22, 19*

FROM 2nd from London # 5747.

"We intend to begin on the first of February unrestricted submarine warfare. We shall endeavor in spite of this to keep the United States of america neutral. In the event of this not succeeding, we make Mexico a proposal of alliance on the following basis: make war together, make peace together, generous financial support and an understanding on our part that Mexico is to reconquer the lost territory in Texas, New Mexico, and Arizona. The settlement in detail is left to you. You will inform the President of the above most secretly as soon as the outbreak of war with the United States of America is certain and add the suggestion that he should, on his own initiative, ~~invite~~ Japan to immediate adherence and at the same time mediate between Japan and ourselves. Please call the President's attention to the fact that the ruthless employment of our submarines now offers the prospect of compelling England in a few months to make peace." Signed, ZIMMERMANN.